Taking Back Your Life

Simple Strategies for Personal Growth

By

Don Loyd

Don Loyd

ISBN-13: 978-1456446437

10 9 8 7 6 5 4 3 2 1

First Edition

What They Say About

Taking Back Your Life

Pearls of Wisdom

Finally, a self-improvement book that delivers what it promises! In his new little gem of a book, Don Loyd distills for you wisdom and life-improvement strategies that are certain to benefit anyone who takes them to heart.

Taking Back Your Life--Simple Strategies for Personal Growth delivers exactly what its title promises. These are not complex strategies that promise sky-in-the-pie wealth and success. Rather they are, as the title states, simple strategies that virtually anyone can use to achieve more success, happiness and contentment in life.

The book is enriched by the inclusion of stories about how star athletes, business people, parents and others have faced challenges and achieved success in their lives. Don also shares touching and memorable stories from his own life showing how he has gracefully and successfully handled challenges and set-backs life has thrown his way.

Whether you are looking for inspiration, strategies for self-improvement or help in finding more meaning in your life, you are certain to find pearls of wisdom that will benefit you in this book.

Donald Moine, Ph.D.
www.DrMoine.com

A Help For Many

I just finished reading <u>Taking Back Your Life - Simple Strategies for Person Growth.</u> As a Sales Staff Recruiter, I found it was simple, powerful and to the point.

Don Loyd's new book should help many people get off the couch and do something about their life to benefit themselves and the people in their lives. This book will be a great addition to the libraries of sales people as well as those looking to improve their mindset.

Steve Tabb, National Director of Recruiting
www.ThePremierAdvantage.com

Opens Possibility Thinking

With the world and our daily lives becoming ever more complex the simplicity of <u>Taking Back Your Life</u> is refreshing. Author, Don Loyd, offers the reader a formula for living a life filled with joy, abundance, creativity and passion.

From the first page to the last are words of wisdom that open up a world of possibility thinking. This book is perfect for anyone going through transition, questioning your purpose and/or simply wanting to live life to the fullest.

Kathleen Gage
The Street Smarts Marketer
www.kathleengage.com

Easy to Implement

I have read and thoroughly enjoyed <u>Taking Back Your Life - Simple Strategies for Person Growth.</u> As a trainer and mental skills expert myself, I read many books to see what I can learn about personal development, I found this was easy to understand, easy to implement and easy to keep on reading! Great book to get you to where you want to be.

Don Loyd's new book should easily help many people get the right *attitude, mindset and motivation, to make for themselves the life they want*!

Loran Northey
www.paramountcoaching.com

An Incredible Book of Encouragement

WOW!!!! Read it and loved it!

As an educator and former pastor I find it hard for so many of us to truly understand the potential power and potential possibilities a person truly has. Don Loyd's "Taking Back Your Life" is an incredible book of encouragement and realistic step-by-step guides to achieving our goals, happiness and life's purpose.

If you can add one new book to your library this year, make it "Taking Back Your Life – Simples Strategies for Personal Development."

Dr. R. Arden Johnson

Something to Sink Your Teeth Into

A knockout!! I have just finished reading Don Loyd's new book "Taking Back Your Life - Simple Strategies for Personal Growth" and it delivers exactly what the title claims.

As a motivational speaker and personal development coach I found his new book both inspiring and a relative blue print for those who desire to turn their life around and start living the life they truly deserve.

I have read much of Don's writings over the years and believe that this may be his best work. He gives anyone with the determination to succeed the rules and guidelines that will surely take them to their dreams. Great job Don! You really have given us something we can sink our teeth into and make the changes we need to make to live the life we desire.

Bruce Kapp
Mr. Motivation
Live the Dream

Books & Audios by Don Loyd

- *The Art of Parenting – How to Produce Achievers*
- *Creating Wealth in Declining Real Estate Markets*
- *Creating Wealth for Women*
- *Creating Wealth Manual*
- *How to Make Your Dreams Come True*
- *How to Buy Your First Home*
- *Real Estate Exit Strategies*
- *The Cure for Declining Income*
- *My New Reality Journal*
- *Marketing and Selling Your Home*
- *A Practical Guide for FSBOs*
- *Earn Amazing Money - Think Your Way to Riches*
- *Oregon Developer's License Manual*
- *90 Day Quick Start Real Estate Investment Manual*
- *How to Create Wealth Through Education* (Audio)
- *Simple Strategies for Personal Growth* (Audio with Shannon Bart, MA)

"A successful man is one who can lay a firm foundation with the bricks others have thrown at him."

David Brinkley

Your Special Bonus

Sign up for . . .

Simple Strategies for Personal Empowerment

This newsletter is one of quotes, encouragement and motivation. Three times each week you will receive positive input and affirmations that will help create a new mindset and transform your life.

Sign up by emailing:

SignMeUp@DonLoyd.com

and type in "Subscribe" in the subject line.

Courtesy of Don Loyd and DreamMaker Press, LLC

"Defeat is not the worst of failures.
Not to have tried is the true failure."

George Edward Woodberry

Table of Contents

Meet My Friend

Don Loyd

My first memory of Don is of a friendly, unassuming gentleman who was gracious and complimentary of those around him. We met at the gym—both part of what we refer to as "the morning gym crowd".

Don and I spoke briefly on a frequent basis. What I have discovered while spending more time with Don is that this seemingly simple person is really a multifaceted and dynamic individual who can be a tough businessman on one hand and yet on the other kind and nurturing.

There is no question that Don is qualified to pass along information on the topic of this book – and give great tips for being successful. His professional resume includes business owner, real estate developer, general contractor, investor, mortgage broker, teacher, writer, author and public speaker.

He can tell you about overcoming difficulties in your life and using your challenges as building blocks for creating a stronger, more fulfilling life. So the question becomes, what qualifies Don to write about overcoming difficulties? As Paul

Harvey as well as Don has so eloquently put it, you have to know "The Rest of the Story."

I want you to go back to your childhood days of lemonade stands, allowances, and piggy banks. Those are some of the things that taught most of us about money and how we place value on things.

Now imagine a seven year old boy knocking on your door, trying to sell you a box of greeting cards—not for the local school or the boy scouts, but for his own individual sense of entrepreneurship.

How could anyone NOT buy those greeting cards? That little boy was Don Loyd. Selling greeting cards is, however, just one example of his determination and work ethic.

He also created a roadside apple stand when he was in the second grade. And he was certainly not afraid to work hard. He got those apples by gathering them with his brother from nearby orchards. I don't know about you but my Mom made my lemonade.

Unfortunately for the Loyd brothers, the apples didn't sell well, but Don was determined to find his gold mine—even at that young age. As he puts it, "The fact that I had failed didn't seem to bother me. I kept thinking and planning". From this, the greeting card sales business was born. Despite his mother's repeat patronage, however, the greeting cards weren't as profitable as he had imagined.

From there he moved on to TV Guide sales, and ultimately the coveted paper route. Now, I want you to imagine being that young boy selling greeting cards, TV Guides®, and delivering papers to houses—but not being able to speak one, clear, intelligible sentence.

Yes—Don had a terrible speech impediment. You would never know it to watch him speak now, but for the majority of his early years he stuttered so badly that there were times people could not understand him. He describes it this way; "My problem made talking difficult and understanding what I was saying almost impossible at times."

As an example of how bad his speech was, when he tried to enlist in the Army, even they rejected him. He states: "This was during the Viet Nam war and they were taking almost any young man with a normally beating heart."

As you might imagine his peers often teased and made fun of him. They made jokes about his stuttering and called him names such as "Stutterin' Don". To make matters worse, his family moved frequently, sometimes up to two times per school year. That meant he had to switch schools and adjust to a new group of kids each time.

It's hard enough to move once when you are growing up, even if you are among the "in" crowd. Knowing that with each move the teasing would start over with fresh ideas and a new group of tormenters must have been Hell.

I remember growing up watching kids who had troubles similar to those that Don experienced. I knew some of them. To this day, I have friends and acquaintances who have never gotten over the emotional scars that they bore as the result of youthful cruelty. These are scars that have a lasting impact on self-esteem, personal feelings of value, and often keep people from believing they can be successful.

Yet Don has far surpassed what even he knew he could accomplish. He is a testament to overcoming hardship, and in fact, looking it square in the eye and charging full speed ahead. Not only has he been successful, but he is successful at the very thing that was once the hardest for him—speaking.

His is a message that is universal in scope and applicable to all of us at varying times in our lives: "As hard as my speech impediment was to endure, I was determined not to let it, or other people's reaction to it, stand in the way of my dreams. I decided I was in charge of my life, not those who poked fun of or ridiculed me. My success, if any, was up to me."

This is the basic principle for our message. Our lives, our dreams, our success, are determined by our choices. We are responsible for creating our own happiness despite what happens to us or what others think of us.

During our conversations, Don expressed to me another very important lesson that he's learned, and that is the relationship between success and significance. Everyone wants to be "successful," but what does that really mean?

Don put it best when he said, "Success is a fickle thing that is defined differently in different cultures and to different people. Significance, on the other hand, is what one does with his or her success. It is about giving to others and contributing to something bigger."

He went on to say, "I would rather be significant than 'successful'." It is this that I find to be the essence of Don.

I will share one final quote from Don to summarize the relationship between success and significance. "If, at the end of your life, there are trophies and money, and world acclaim, you may be considered successful. If you leave something greater than you are that carries on, you may be described as significant."

I count it a privilege to know Don, and to have learned from him. I am honored that he considers me a colleague. He is a shining example of overcoming struggles, and he has a fantastic formula for success. I hope that you will not only learn from his experience, but also enjoy being a part of his significance.

Shannon Bart, MA (Psychology)
Health Coach

Introduction

This book began in 2009. I was on the management and training team of a national sales and marketing organization that recruited financial services sales reps.

Knowing that many of the new people had experienced financial challenges as the result of the failing economy, I wrote articles in my newsletter that would build them up and assist in the development of a change in mindset.

I wanted to replace negative thinking with positive input. What you read in this book is, in part, some of the ideas I shared with our sales and management staff – a philosophy that I have espoused for the last 40 years.

You will find some repetition in this book. That happens for a reason. Some important points need to be repeated in different settings, and a slight change in verbiage, in order for the lessons to be learned by the largest number of people.

You may also note that there is a lack of bundling similar thoughts into sections. I did that because I want to surprise you. I want you to eagerly turn the pages to see what nugget you find next – as though you are on a treasure hunt. The nature of this book lends itself to that approach.

My goal is to motivate you toward greater success regardless of where you are right now, or where you want to go tomorrow. I have done my best to keep the strategies simple and straight forward.

I've shared personal information about how I have dealt with success, failure, hurts, and more. These true stories are to illustrate that I have faced my own challenges and moved forward. I'm not a person who simply writes about a life changing philosophy. I live it, and have for five decades.

There are lots of good motivational speakers and writers, and I encourage you to read and listen to what they have to say. Becoming the person you are meant to be is a process and each of us have something to add to help make your life more full.

When you are finished with this book, I hope you have the tools you need to:

1. Replace a negative mindset with a positive one
2. Look forward rather than focus on the past
3. Discover your purpose for living
4. Succeed in your personal, business, family and spiritual life
5. Find abundant living
6. Find peace

All of these are achievable goals. Do you think you can enjoy the above? If you think you can, you're right. If you think you can't, you are also right. It's really up to you.

Success or Mediocrity?

The difference between break through success and mediocrity is largely one of mindset. Your mindset will form and nurture personal boundaries you will not readily want to traverse.

The purpose of this book is to get you past your comfort zone and move you forward in your relationships, spiritual growth, business endeavors, family life, and more. In fact, I want you to experience success in ALL areas of your life.

The key to much of your success is found in the way you view life challenges and your overall outlook on life. Is your glass half full or half empty? Or maybe you think the glass has toppled and there's nothing left?

Are you ready to take back your life? The simple ideas expressed within the pages of this powerful book will help you realize that goal.

My hope for you is very simple: I want you to enjoy life, be blessed by it, and live it to the fullest.

Here's to your Success.

Don Loyd

If we are ever in doubt about what to do,

it is a good rule to ask ourselves what we

shall wish on the morrow that we had done.

John Lubbock

1

What Others Think About You

I begin this book with a foundational issue that affects all of us. It can be argued that we are pre-wired to respond to the pressure of others. In some ways, that pressure helps form societal norms and mores.

On the other hand, when that pressure questions your value as a human being, you better start questioning the validity of the bearer of the pressure. Let's start with a question:

What is the value of someone's opinion of your ability and personal worth? When we were teenagers, most of us wanted the acceptance of our peers. As a result, it mattered a great deal and we wanted to conform (non-conformists conform to the mores of other non-conformists!).

By the time we were in our late 30s and 40s we said we didn't much care what "they" thought. But by then our lives were molded as we tried to live up to the (sometimes) impossible standards.

Now I find that what was really important at age 20 does not register on any scale of importance I now embrace. The time I spent thinking about what other people thought about me was, for me, truly a waste of time. On top of that, I've learned they really didn't spend too much time thinking about me anyway.

Today when someone has an unsolicited opinion of me that I find objectionable, I simply think, "That person is rather presumptuous, isn't he/she?"

The life you are living is _**yours**_. So find purpose and live it to the fullest. What others think about you will not pay your bills or produce wonderful relationships - nor does what they think really matter!

Just remember the value of someone's unsolicited opinion of you is worth every penny you paid for it!

If you're interested, here's my advice:

1. Find objective truth (as opposed to subjective truth) in which to adhere and serve as an anchor for your life and life's work.

2. Be yourself! Along your journey in self development, set goals that accomplish things you believe important.

3. As stated in the body of this chapter, find purpose in your life and live it. You are here for a reason. Why are you here?

4. Regardless of the nay-sayers, embrace and apply principles that build your personal character and help define the person you want to be.

5. Make time for meditation and reflection. In our fast pace society, this time is needed so we can reconnect with our values and moral compass.

6. Truly realize that success is not accomplished in a vacuum. We need other people in our lives. With that recognition, we can learn to give of ourselves to others who are less fortunate than we are.

7. When you fail to live up to your ideal standards, and you will on occasion, recognize the failure, make adjustments, and then simply move forward. Here's how one first century thinker dealt with the issue of moving forward in his personal life:

> "But this one thing I do--forgetting everything which is past and stretching forward to what lies in front of me, with my eyes fixed on the goal I push on to secure the prize . . ."

Now, go make it a great day by focusing on the "prize" – regardless of what "others" have to say about it.

Learn from yesterday, live for today, hope for tomorrow. The important thing is not to stop questioning.

Albert Einstein

2

The Challenge of Change

Change (sometimes called challenges, disappointments, failures, and the like), in our lives is something most of us tend to avoid. Change is hard whether in personal relationships, business, politics, or finances – whatever.

In my real estate business, change is never ending. Whenever I get something figured out, or a new loan program is introduced, I make adjustment and plan to move forward. I take a couple of steps in that direction, and the rules change and I start over. It can be very frustrating if I allow it to be.

It's like the bird struggling to break out of an egg shell. It's hard to break out and there's a struggle, but how will the bird learn to fly in its shell? The option for the bird is to either hatch or die.

In reality, the only constant is change. We are in a state of flux until we die. Although facing changes head-on is like swimming against a river's current, the benefit is that the process, while painful at times, sharpens our senses and makes us stronger as we struggle to adjust. Yes, it would be much easier to simply go with the flow, but any dead fish can do that and who wants to be a dead fish?

The struggle that comes from the emotional, psychological and physical effects of change is necessary to go forward and grow stronger. If you don't move forward, you will move backward – there is no staying the same. It's the struggle that enables you to achieve the next level.

Don't be a dead fish that floats with the current (death) or a bird that won't break free of its shell and only wished it could fly (slavery). The goal is to look at change with expectancy (positive mental attitude) and embrace the opportunities that will come to you as a result of enduring the pain of breaking free from the challenge of change.

Living is a grand experience. Embracing change will make it possible for you to learn life lessons and live life to the fullest.

Now, it's up to you. Go create an amazing day.

3

It's OK - Swing Away

One of the greatest hitters in baseball history is Mickey Mantle who is remembered as a great home run slugger, but did you know he struck out more than 1,750 times? In addition, he walked to first base more than 1,750 times. In other words, there were more than 3,500 times he went to home plate and didn't hit the ball. That's the equivalent of seven full seasons he never had a base hit!

Here's the lesson: it's not the misses that count, it's the hits. Learn from your misses but focus on your hits.

When I make a mistake I increase my awareness and improve my performance. I refuse to relegate my disappointments and failures to the back of the bus and purposefully move them up front where I can deal with them, work out the kinks, make adjustments and get back on track toward success. I turn my mistakes and failures into stepping stones toward my goal. I figure if I didn't make a mistake yesterday, I didn't learn much.

If you want to enjoy success in your personal life and business, and overcome the invisible handicaps that are detrimental to that success, step in the batter's box and strike out a few times. It's okay – <u>never fear failure!</u>

Here's how you step up to the plate:

1. Decide what it is you want to do and carve out a niche for yourself. If you try to be all things to all people, the deck is stacked against you. You have to find a unique position for you.

2. Set some measurable goals. You need both long term and short term measurable goals. Write these goals out on paper. Until you write them down, they simply do not exist.

3. Define how you will attain those goals. Write a step-by-step plan that clearly defines how you are going to reach your destination.

4. Work your plan. As you do the daily activity it takes to accomplish your goals, focus on that activity rather than the goal. If your goal is to purchase one rehab property each month, focus on the activity that will result in that one purchase.

5. Make adjustments as needed. When a mistake is made determine where you went wrong and readjust your approach but <u>do not </u>allow yourself to become distracted from achieving your goals.

6. As you work your plan, start thinking about ways to give to others. If you cannot give away your money, it owns you. You will become self-focused and shallow and contentment will always elude you.

7. Be a mentor to others. There are millions of people who would like to be where you are. Take one or two along for the ride with you.

The question you now face is crucial. What are you going to do with this information? My advice is to swing away. Strike out, make some adjustments – most of all enjoy the ride. Life can and should be a thrilling experience, but it's up to you to make it happen.

Today, get in the batter's box and swing.

And, make it an astonishing day.

Batter up!

Life is like a coin. You can spend it any way you wish,
but you only spend it once.
Lillian Dickson

4

Power in Taking Action

To achieve a level of success, and hopefully significance, you need to create a precise plan detailing exactly what you must do in order to realize your dream. You will have to make adjustments to your plan as you go forward, but if you don't write is down, how will you know if you are making progress toward the goal? Be sure, too, to set a timetable for the completion of your tasks. Open-ended tasks seem always to be pushed to the rear of the priorities.

Breakdown your objectives into daily activities and then manage those activities. You'll be surprised at how easy it is to complete a lot of work when you manage your time well. Don't let the phone, walk-in customers or whatever "emergencies" may present themselves rule your life. Also, as best as you can, resist the urge to put off doing the things that need to get done. Take Charge!

During certain hours, I refuse to take phone calls. I let them go to voice mail and return them when I arrive at the allotted time. I used to have a script on my voice mail that said, "Thanks for calling. I have several appointments today. I can return your call between 10 and 11 AM or 3 to 4 PM. Please let me know when the best time for you would be." That simple script gave me back my life.

When you write down your list of daily tasks, post the list where you can easily see it. You will find the more you look at it, the more likely you will be to accomplish the tasks you've set. And importantly, I find that it helps to deal with difficult things first. Get anything distasteful or disagreeable off your plate as soon as you can so you can enjoy the rest of the day.

Thomas Carlyle, the 9th Century Scottish essayist, wrote: "Men do less than they ought, unless they do all they can." If you fail to take action, you will fail in reaching your target. Do all you can!

Define what you want to accomplish (as best as you can at this point) and do the daily activity that's needed to get you where you want to go. Practice focusing on the daily activity – not necessarily the end goal. The action you implement will get you to the finish line. There is power in taking action.

It's up to you now. I suggest that if you fail to take action today, you will be in the same place this time next year. The main difference between dreamers and doers is very simple. Doers take action.

Make it a "Take Action" kind of day. What do you have to lose?

5

Going Forward With Physical Limitations

If you want to succeed in every area in your life, ou have to take an active role in your own future: don't allow others to dictate your success. Sometimes this means working past, through or around a disadvantage, such as a physical limitation.

To use the sports analogy I used in chapter 3, you have to step up to the plate, lift your bat over your shoulder, and take a swing. I introduced you to home run hitter Mickey Mantle, center fielder and first baseman for the Yankees in the fifties and sixties.

Whenever "the Mick" strolled to home plate to take his turn at bat, people paid attention, knowing they might see him hit a ball out of the park for a home run. What most people don't realize, however, is that Mickey Mantle held the record for the most strike-outs: he failed at bat more than any other professional baseball player. Yet what we remember are his successes.

The same thing can happen to you: keep getting into the "batter's box" and swinging... hit a home run or even a base hit now and again, and people won't remember your failures. They will remember the times you scored.

If you are living a life as a spectator, you aren't getting in the batter's box. You're not even sitting in the dugout. People who use excuses for sitting out limit themselves by their attitudes.

Here's a couple of examples of people who got in the game and struck out a few times:

I know of a real estate broker in a wheelchair who earns six figures each and every year. He figured out a way to sell real estate without picking people up in his car and showing them property: he does it all by mail, email and fax from the comfort of his office. He targets out-of-state owners and lists their property for sale.

There is a general contractor in California who is in much the same position. He pulls up to a job in his truck and never gets out of it. He can't. He can't walk!

A man in our church owned and operated a successful restaurant. He had once owned a profitable tire re-capping business. One day, while working at his plant, a tire blew up in his face and blinded him. Steel plates were put in his face. He wasn't able to return to the work he knew, so, in his forties, he opened a restaurant. I've seen him stand at the cashier's box and make change for his customers.

I became a general contractor when it became apparent that I could no longer work construction. One day, nailing shakes on a roof outside of Santa Rosa, California, I bent down to plug in my skill saw so I could cut a hip roof. As soon as I connected the cord to the saw, I was thrown off the roof. There was short in the wiring. I broke three vertebrae in the fall. I was flat on my back for a time and when I recovered, I found I had neither the strength nor the stamina to do the work I had previously done. For years, I lived with chronic pain.

I'd been pulled off of the playing field. But I didn't stop playing: I learned how to play a different position in the same of game. In the process I stopped working for hourly pay (which is a sure fire plan for just getting by) and began making very serious money and receiving positive recognition from others.

Rather than presenting a stop sign, a handicap or disability can be your ticket to great things. If life gives you lemons, rejoice in the lemons and find a way to sell lemonade. I've read many stories of penniless immigrants coming to this country and becoming millionaires. If someone can go from rags to riches speaking broken English, you can do it with a handicap or disability.

Enough about other people - here's how you can succeed:

   1. Think about all the things you can do and make a list of them. Decide what you want to do, and find a niche.

   2. Set some measurable goals, both long- and short-term.

   3. Define how you will attain those goals, and write a plan. You must have a road map directing you to your destination.

   4. Your plan must include an activity for each day. Do the daily activity. Focus on it, rather than the goal.

   5. Make adjustments as needed.

6. Be a mentor to others. A ton of folk would like to be where you are. Take one or two along for the ride with you, and teach them what you have learned.

7. Learn to give. In order to have a complete, balanced and fulfilled life, you have to learn to give some of your time and some of your money to something greater than yourself and your bank account. He with the largest list of assets at death is not the winner. If you can't learn to give, you are controlled by your possessions - a very sad and lonely way to live.

Remember, if you don't make it happen, it won't happen. Get in the game!

Make it a "Going Forward" kind of day.

6

Making Mistakes – A Part of Living

Imagine a world where scientists fail to act for fear of making a mistake. Did you know that many of the cures and treatments for illnesses we benefit from today are directly due to the failure of great minds? They were searching for one thing, failed, and discovered something else.

We all make mistakes. The key question you have to ask yourself is, how will you handle them? Will you allow them to discourage you and generate fear in your life? Or, will you take advantage of them, learn important confidence building lessons, and move forward?

I believe the positive and healthy way to address blunders is to address them head-on by not blaming others and taking personal responsibility. I challenge you to stand up and courageously say, "This is my responsibility and I will learn from my error."

If you will do this, the opportunity to gain important information that will hasten the achievement of your goal will come your way. Please make no mistake here (pun intended), you only learn from a mistake after you admit you have made one. Only then can you truly replace the fear of moving forward with confidence.

One sign of a healthy attitude toward mistakes is the ability to smile at them. When you can laugh at your mistakes, you are more likely to learn from them than beat yourself up over them. When that happens, you have also arrived at a place where you no longer judge yourself on the basis of a single event or two.

Your progress in this area may be a straight line. But if you keep learning, as a result of your mistakes, you will have more success than failures.

Will you make mistakes? If you don't try anything, you will not. But if you want success, you certainly will. Albert Einstein said, "The only sure way to avoid making mistakes is to have no new ideas."

As Thomas Edison said regarding his many failures in trying to create the light bulb, "I have discovered 999 ways that won't work." You and I should relentlessly pursue that spirit.

Never fear what others might say or think. If you fail, you will learn valuable lessons which will lead to your success. It's okay to fail.

This is your day. Make it a grand one. It's up to you.

7

Making Adjustments –
A Part of Life

Over the years I have learned that the best made plans will need adjustments. There will always be unforeseen circumstances arising in your business, personal and spiritual goals. I have started several businesses and it has been very unusual when I didn't have to make adjustments.

The reason we have to adjust is, we don't always know all we need to know before we set out on a quest to reach a goal. We *think* we know what we're doing, but that is hardly ever the case. There is always something to tweak in order to increase production or responses, create more cash flow or enjoy a better result, etc.

Those who find it hard to think "outside the box" find us "what box?" kind of thinkers difficult to understand. I know people, like you do, who simply cannot adjust to changes. But change we must because there is no standing still. We are either going forward or backward. If not, then we are drying up and slowly dying.

At one time whale oil fueled our lighting fixtures. When was the last time you purchased whale oil? Better options came along and those in the whale oil business that couldn't, or wouldn't, change, found themselves in economic peril. My grandfather used horses and horse drawn wagons as a means of transportation. But I haven't seen anyone in my lifetime riding a horse into town to visit his banker.

Change is a constant. You will have to make adjustments in your life to focus on reaching the success you want. In order to make the time you need, you may have to cut back on or even give up certain activities. The trick is to prioritize.

Surround yourself with people who want you to succeed and avoid negative thinkers (they will bring you down rather than you building them up). Build a master mind group of four or five people who are successful and can share positive ideas about your success interests.

Most of all, don't resist change and the adjustments you have to make - embrace it and the adjustments. Most change is out of your control. What you can control, however, is how you deal with change and the mental mindset that's needed to succeed. You can view life with all its challenges as a wonderful treasure hunt. The question is, will you?

Now go make it a terrific day as you find power in adjusting to changing environments.

8

The Power of Personal Focus

Here's a fundamental truth: You can only think about one thing at a time. What you spend your time thinking about will form your mindset, and shape your world view.

If you constantly think about the negative, you will be a negative person and people will shy away from you. If you choose to be positive you will find people being drawn to you.

Successful people tend to be positive thinkers. They see the glass as half full rather than half empty. They look for the good in situations, especially those things that might be discouraging and disappointing.

With every bad experience there is a positive side - your job is to find it. It's like the two young brothers who were put into separate rooms filled with only horse manure. One child sat and cried because there was nothing but manure in the room. The other child was elatedly flinging manure all over the ceiling and walls. He knew with that much manure in the room there had to be a pony - and he was looking for it and expected to find it!

Those for whom life has evolved into a treasure hunt will focus on the positive. Every situation has both negative and positive aspects but as I previously stated, you can only give thought to one thing at a time. Focus on the positive and live life with expectancy. It's a choice you are free to make.

There have been many bad experiences in my life. I even came close to death on one occasion. But I have done my best to find the good in the bad.

Embossed on my brain are the words of my doctor declaring in a troubled voice, "Don, you could be dead within minutes." The first available surgeon was located and I was rushed into surgery.

While recovering from open heart surgery, as soon as the fog of anesthesia worn off, I thought, "how can I turn this into a positive?" In my hospital room with limited movement, I began writing an article comparing the goal of checking out of the hospital to business success.

I entitled that article, "Stepping Stones to Success" and included it in my book "Creating Wealth for Women." The result of a bad experience for me resulted in the encouragement of many people. I found the pony.

Now, it's your turn. Focus on finding your pony.

Make it a great pony finding day.

9

Confronting Your Fears

Many people never really try to succeed because they fear failure. I'll let you in on a secret: it's okay to fail. I've learned some of my most important lessons through failure. It is true that some fear is healthy. It is crucial to remember, however, to keep your fears and worries in perspective: if you let them overwhelm you, they may rob you of your dreams.

Successful entrepreneurs, and those who live life to the fullest, refuse to let worry, fear and uncertainty hold them back from reaching their goals and realizing their potential. I want the same for you.

I challenge you to eliminate from your vocabulary words like *if, can't, never, won't,* etc. Don't say, *"If I'd had a better childhood, I could've_____"* or, *"I can't _____. I'm not smart or good looking enough."*

Don't think things like:
> *"I'm such a jerk. How could I have said that?"*
> *"I'm a loser. I'll never get anywhere."*

- ➤ *"I'm so stupid. I should have learned this by now."*
- ➤ *"I don't fit in. I don't belong with these people."*
- ➤ *"I'll never be good enough. I'll never do it right."*
- ➤ *"I'm permanently emotionally damaged. I'll never be okay."*
- ➤ *"No one could love me. I'm not lovable."*

Those kinds of words, and that kind of thinking, will almost certainly become self-fulfilling prophecies that will take you down a path away from where you want to go. Replace them with positive affirmations – restated in terms that reinforce positive behavior and a positive mindset.

Try these:
"I know I can do it."
"I am as capable as anyone else."
"I have my own special talents and abilities."
"I'll stick with this as long as it takes."
"I'm a great person!"

These positive affirmations, especially when spoken frequently, will result in a new reality. You will see yourself in a new light. Just remember: whatever you think about yourself as it relates to success and achieving your dreams is true.

Now, go look fear in the eye and walk right through it. Here's to superb, magnificent day. It is your choice.

Create a fantastic day.

10

Embracing Challenges

We all face challenges that test our resolve. Often a challenge will stop us dead in our tracks. We hit a roadblock and our forward motion ceases. The goal, then, is to face such challenges with resolve and persistence in order to turn them into opportunities so we can continue forward.

Challenges can be viewed as an exciting ride. They can turn life into a treasure hunt or a grand adventure because you never know what you're going to find tomorrow.

If I come up against a brick wall, I try to find the crack in the mortar or a hidden door I can open that will enable me to press on. Sometimes I have to go around the wall, and that's okay, too. It's still a journey worth taking.

I used to pray for challenges. I loved the opportunity to do what "they" said couldn't be done. If someone told me I couldn't, I had to prove him or her wrong. It was like saying to a dog, "Sic 'em." I would charge out and do the undoable. (One day my wife asked me not to pray for anymore challenges. She told me she didn't know if she could go along for the ride anymore!)

Determination and resolve are the two things that separate those who succeed in realizing their dreams from those who don't. Once you have a vision of where you want to go, resolve - *firmly* - to get there.

Now it's your choice! Will you run from the challenge that you now face? Or, will you have the courage to view it as an opportunity for success and a satisfied life?

Norman Vincent Peale reminds us, "Action is a great restorer and builder of confidence. Inaction is not only the result, but the cause, of fear. Perhaps the action you take will be successful; perhaps different action or adjustments will have to follow. But any action is better than no action at all."

Go make it a magnificent day.

11

Creating Miracles

Bob Richards was a world class athlete. In fact, he made three Olympic teams (48' Bronze Medal, 52' Gold Medal, and 56' Gold Medal) competing in the decathlon and pole vaulting. He was the second man to pole vault 15 feet, and is the only two-time Olympic gold medal winner in the pole vault.

Richards understood that what many call miracles is the direct result of rolling up your shirt sleeves, focusing on a goal, and then working at achieving the goal.

Richards declared: *"I won it, at least five million times. Men who were stronger, bigger and faster than I was could have done it, but they never picked up a pole, and never made the feeble effort to pick their legs off the ground and get over the bar."*

Therein lies the difference between those who do, and those who just talk about doing; the successful "pick up the pole, and lift their legs off the ground." They take action by going through the exercise of doing!

Richards is right. It's not about who's he strongest, smartest, most talented, most gifted, best looking, best dressed or has the most potential. These advantages will get you no where if you don't back them up with action.

I've met plenty of people who had all of the above but only skimmed through life without any memorable achievements.

Do you want a miracle in your marriage or other relationships? If you do, clearly define a goal, get some education (i.e., learn the ingredients to a good marriages and relationships) and do the exercises and work needed to reach the goal.

Do you want a miracle in your professional life? Take the same steps. Set a clearly defined goal, gather and assimilate the information you need and then take action.

Creating a "miracle" really is as easy as 1, 2, 3 and 4. But it is also hard. It will take effort on your part. You have to <u>do something</u> that takes you one step closer to your goal.

When you take the first step toward your goal, an interesting thing happens. You don't have to control or manipulate others in order to achieve it. Others, more likely than not, **will follow you**. You become the leader - and believe me, people want to find a leader to follow.

Want a miracle? Here's how to do it.

1. Embrace integrity and develop character.

2. Add a good dose of courage to the mix. (Yes, you can do it!!)

3. Get to work and take action. First by gathering the information you need, making adjustments as needed, and then stepping out to accomplish your "miracle."

4. Enjoy finding the power (and secret) of seeing a "miracle."

Now, go find your "miracle."

When one door of happiness closes,

another opens;

But often we look so long at the closed

door that we do not see the one that has

been opened for us.

Helen Keller

12

Procrastination Be Gone

I can't say this enough: you can have the best plan in the world, but if you don't take action and follow through on it, you simply have a dream – something vague and illusive. Do you talk, and talk, and talk, or plan and plan and plan, but never <u>do</u> anything to get your idea moving? Self-motivated people refuse to procrastinate and are rewarded with the success we all aspire to.

Procrastination strangles the life out of your ideas. It gets you off the coveted bull's eye of completing a goal and you get lost in the maze of planning. Now, there is nothing wrong with planning, we have to do it. But when all you do is plan, you still haven't made any tangible progress, and certainly no money.

According to an article by Hara Estroff Marano in "Psychology Today," about 20% of the population is chronic procrastinators. Psychologist William Knaus estimated that 90% of college students procrastinate. These numbers suggest to me that procrastination is a learned behavior. If it is learned, then it is possible for people to be re-trained.

Here's what I suggest for procrastinators who want to "unlearn" the behavior:

1. Regardless of what your goal is (write a book, build a house, achieve sales goals – whatever), write down your objective. We will call this the mountain top.

2. Define how you want to accomplish your goal - the path to the top of the mountain.

3. The key to achieving your goal is found in reducing your goal to daily activity. In other words, we don't have to reach the summit today, we simply have to take the first step upward.

4. Stop talking about it and do the daily activity. If it's going to take 300 walking steps to reach the top, take the three or four steps today that's needed. Just focus on "today's" three or four steps.

5. Celebrate each day's success! Reaching the summit is the result of following through with your daily activity.

Now, go make it a profitable day.

13

Clout in Catching an Idea

Have you ever had an "aha" kind of idea? The kind that sent electric shock waves tingling through your body? That excited you to the point of wanting to shout it from a mountain top!

A writer acquaintance of mine says it like this: *"Good ideas pop up like fireflies on a June night."* I think most of us have those kinds of moments. An idea pops into your mind as someone is speaking (or you are driving, or reading, or..._____) But the real question is, what do we do with them? The truly successful write those ideas down, do their due diligence and take action.

Fuller argues that the difference between success and failure is dependent upon what you do with an idea within 24 hours of the creative idea. I agree. Just this morning I had a mental light switch on. I got so excited I thought I would burst if I didn't tell someone on my success team about it. Only trouble was, I had the idea at 4:00 AM and my friends were sleeping.

Here's what I did:

- Wrote down the idea (until you have it on paper it really does not exist!).

- Pulled out my calculator and did some rudimentary math to try to determine if it was a valid idea and whether I would receive a good return for my time and creativity.

- Concluded I would earn a significant return on my investment of time and start up costs.

- Identified a specific market niche.

- Wrote a statement, in bullet points, about what I wanted the new idea to do for my buyer niche. This will be the basic outline for my promotional material.

- Considered a marketing approach.

- Identified possible success team members who could help make this idea a reality.

- Spent the millions of dollars I was going to make (just kidding).

- Next, I will make adjustments as I further explore my new, exciting idea.

I think you get the point! Taking action is the key that unlocks the proverbial door to success however you define it. Until you take action on a creative idea, it will vanish, as quickly as a firefly light, and you will soon forget it. It will surface later, of course, when you see someone else had the same idea. You will react like I have in the past: "If only I would have ....."

When your next idea comes up, capture it as quickly as you would a firefly. Write it down, think it through and do something about it. If you don't, your idea will be gone as quickly as it appeared.

Now, catch a firefly and make it a super creative day!

14

PMA –The Secret Ingredient

Have you ever noticed how refreshing it is to be around people who look at life with expectation? Not only do they cheer you up but they cheer you on. They give you input to encourage your success.

Two of the most valuable keys to success that I can share with you is to:

1. Surround yourself with people who have a positive mindset and,

2. Become one of those people yourself. Train yourself to look on the bright side regardless of what you're facing. There are always reasons to be thankful, to have a positive mindset.

There's an old Persian proverb that's appropriate here: "I had the blues because I had no shoes until upon the street, I met a man who had no feet."

It's about mindset and perspective. Evaluate your strengths and weaknesses objectively and then go forward. When self-doubt surfaces because you don't have "shoes," be thankful that you have "feet:" and move forward.

When self-doubt raises its ugly head, ask these two questions:

- ✓ Did I give my best effort to today's activities?
- ✓ Did I move closer to reaching my goals?

If the answer is "yes," yippee - go celebrate with a reward of some kind. If it isn't, though, don't kick yourself. Ask, "why not?" and do things differently tomorrow. Bring to mind positive affirmations and stay thankful for the things you do enjoy.

Here's my challenge to you - Find something positive to say to everyone you meet today and be a blessing to others. You will be surprised how much better you will feel by being kind and using words that build up others.

Now, go make it a super positive day. Find at least three things for which you can be thankful. There's incredible power in owning a positive mental mindset.

15

Success by Embracing Enthusiasm

Enthusiasm is rarely a topic that comes to mind when we think of success. And yet, without it, life becomes mundane and the spark we wish to ignite in others fizzles away without the desired result.

Embracing enthusiasm is important because it replaces fear and worry. When I was in my early 40s I experienced what many call a mid-life crisis. Prior to this dark, short chapter in my life, I was accustomed to making decisions on a huge scale. I spiraled downward into a period of depression in which I could not decide on the color of my socks each morning.

The catalyst for my turn-around was the new project I tepidly decided to take on. Early in the process, enthusiasm was a quality I forced on myself. I pretended I had it until it finally showed up. It showed up because (I think), as others became excited about my dream, their excitement spilled over to me and replaced pretending enthusiasm with the real thing.

I grew into a bona fide, honest cheerleader for finding success in every "today." That was the end of "bad days" for me. Now there are good days and, better yet, great days! And an interesting thing happened: my enthusiasm and excitement became contagious. Others reflected my newly refashioned positive mindset. The spark I sought to ignite became a forest fire from which many lives were positively impacted.

Here's my advice to you if you want to enjoy success and are having a tough time getting excited:

> ➤ Fake enthusiasm until it becomes real (no, you will not be a phony)

> ➤ Surround yourself with positive people (don't listen to negative talk)

> ➤ Think about how you can help others less fortunate than you (gets the focus off you and on someone else - which is a great thing for your well being)

> ➤ Learn how to give yourself and some of your money to others (if you refuse to give, then the things you own and the money you possess **OWNS you**.

Norman Vincent Peale states, "Often enthusiasm is the bridge between poverty and prosperity." I know, from personal experience, he's right.

He also wrote: "Enthusiasm releases the drive to carry you over obstacles and adds significance to all you do."

Now it's up to you. What will you do with this information? File it away in some dark corner, or get excited about your dreams and go for them? It's your choice.

Now, go make it an enthusiastically great day.

16

The Influence of a Dream

Born into slavery in 1822, Harriet Tubman had a dream of freeing her people from slavery. She risked her life many times during a ten year period to help free people along the Underground Railroad, a secret network of safe houses where runaway slaves could stay on their journey north to freedom. Harriet Tubman realized her dream and you can realize yours, too. Here's step one:

Clearly define the vision of what you want to accomplish.

If you don't know what it is that you want, how will you know when you've arrived? The more distinct your dream becomes, and the better you articulate it, the faster you'll achieve it.

I want you to try an experiment. Put your feet flat on the floor with your back straight. Now, relax and close your eyes. I want you to picture success, whatever that is to you. I want you to explore the benefits and pleasure of that success. I want you to feel the exhilaration of it. Taste it, smell it.

Now determine to make that vision of success your reality. This new reality can be extended and enlarged upon as you make progress, but without first visualizing your definition of success, you'll never achieve it.

In my 2006 book, <u>My New Reality Journal</u>, I encourage you to dream. I want you to have huge, expansive dreams. And I want you to clearly see where you're going.

Start today by <u>specifically</u> defining what it is you want to accomplish. Don't cheat yourself by stating your dream in general terms such as, "I want to earn a million dollars" or "I want a successful marriage." State your goal in clear terms that will force you to identify your dream.

For example, you might want to state it like this: "In my role as a trusted financial advisor, I will earn a million dollars by working smart while providing my clients the best products available from which they will receive a competitive return on their investment with no exposure of risk."

In that one statement you are including the steps you need to realize your dream. You've stated your beginning point (become a trusted financial advisor) and your ending point (becoming a millionaire) and the steps in between (establish a good reputation, work smart, provide excellent product for your clients and protect them from risk).

What is your dream? Today write it in a simple, clearly defined way. Now, full speed ahead. As the Nike commercial commands, "Just Do It!" And do it now!

17

Goodbye Dad

My father passed from this life to the next on October 15, 2009 - two days after his 62nd wedding anniversary with my mother. Mother ate an anniversary dinner in the hospital cafeteria with my brother and sister while Dad lay in ICU plugged into machines helping him breath and tracking his vital signs.

I didn't think Dad's death would affect me; he had been in very poor health for the last twenty years of his life. The affects of 8 or 9 strokes, 6 or 7 heart attacks, diabetes and a series of bouts with pneumonia had ravished a once strong, articulate, engaging man into a shell of his former self from which he no longer could control his bodily functions or carry on a charming conversation. I assumed his death, when it occurred, would be a welcome relief.

When his death became reality, the emotion I felt caught me off-guard. I spent time pondering his life, legacy and impact. I recalled good times as a child and with relish embraced those warm and loving thoughts. I also remembered the times as a teenager I thought he must not be too bright. I remember thinking one time when I was about 15 years of age: How did someone so stupid grow to be so old (he was in his late 30s)? Later I realized it was I who didn't know very much.

Dad was never a man to say, "I love you," but I knew he did. I reminisced about him walking with me the night I received my bachelors degree. He told me, arm-in-arm, how proud he was of me. Dad never completed the ninth grade and I was the first in the family to earn a degree. After I earned a Doctorate, I heard him tell a friend, "That's my son, Dr. Loyd." I knew he was proud of the accomplishment.

My father was a child of the Great Depression. That event, and subsequent meager living conditions, shaped his world view. The financial and life style choices he made over the course of his life were a direct result of the depression era mindset - work hard and save your money. He always tried to pay his bills in cash and didn't hold bankers in very high regard.

At the age of 14, he quit school to help care for his parents and much younger sister when his father was diagnosed with tuberculosis - a death sentence in many cases in the 1940s. With the help of his two brothers my father worked to provide for the family while my grandfather was confined to an iron lung, Dad and his bothers even purchased a home for their parents during my grandfather's slow recovery from a surgery that left him with the use of half of one lung.

If I remember correctly, they paid couple of thousand dollars for a very small two bedroom home (about four or five hundred square feet) with no indoor plumbing. Those skimpy living quarters became a home that was blessed to have Loyds within the walls for about 40 years (when I was a child my dad added on a full bathroom and extra "indoor porch" so my grandparents would not have to go outside to do the laundry or use the bathroom).

More often than not, that little house was filled with laughter and love as aunts, uncles and boat loads of cousins flocked there for Christmas most of my early years.

There are many other things that rushed to my mind as I considered the life of my dad. I'm a result of his example, leadership and parenting. He helped instill in a positive work ethic and the notion that my word should be my bond. Was my dad perfect? No, he was just a man, and a flawed man at that. He was a person much like you and me.

But he had a huge, caring heart. After my siblings and I were grown, he and Mom took on a second family. At a time when many empty nesters were thinking about retirement and taking off on an RV jaunt, Dad and Mom heard about a family of three pre-teen children needing a foster home. They willingly took on that responsibility and for the next ten or twelve years my parents became their parents - to the point the children eventually changed their names to Loyd and called my parents Dad and Mom. In all, my parents unselfishly opened their hearts and home to a total of five boys and girls needing help.

As I thought about his life, I remember that I missed him as a child. I wished he'd had more time for ball games, camping trips, fishing and hunting adventures. But he was busy providing a roof and meals for his family - a noble and honest thing.

Considering his life as a whole, he touched hundreds, if not thousands, of lives in a positive way and I'm thankful for his leadership, life lessons and love. As I pondered Dad's life I wanted to have some take away value for you. Here's what I came away with:

If you want to make your life count in the eyes of your children and grandchildren, don't allow your business to control your life. Take charge and make the conscious choice to spend time with them. Show them love. Give them memories that money cannot provide. When it comes your time to pass, many of the things you now think important are not very important at all.

Dad was a good man. Some might even argue he was great.

I love you Dad. I will see you later.

18

Success or Significance?

I write and teach a lot about success. I believe success, to a large degree, is our choice. We can accomplish great things if we follow a system, break the system down into daily activity and then manage that activity.

I also enjoy a level of success. There are hundreds of people who look to me as a role model and mentor. I get calls and email messages across the United States from people who desire to do what I do. In one way it's very flattering - in another it's very sobering.

Success, for the sake of success, is not the end game. Here's why: success is fickle. It has no loyalties. Success has no clear definition. It means different things in different cultures and to different people. What may be success to me is mediocrity to someone else. Success is elusive - it is always just a little beyond where you currently are.

More important than success is significance. When setting your goals think beyond mere success; set your eyes on achieving significance. Why? Because success is a narrow field of accomplishment - a "me" mentality with limited impact. Seeking significance broadens the playing field, widens your opportunities and assures a positive impact on others. I desire to be significant more than I desire success.

By using the word "significant" I mean to convey the idea of being "meaningful." Several years ago I came face to face with my own immortality. I was literally seconds away from death. It changed everything for me! I no longer want to achieve goals simply to reach the top - wherever or whatever that is. I want to leave a meaningful legacy. I want to positively impact other lives. I want the world to be a better place because of my contribution, if possible.

It's what one does with success (and I'm not only talking about accumulating large sums of money or climbing some subjective, elusive ladder) that makes the difference between the two. If you truly want your life to count, to achieve significance, I believe you must first learn to give to others. Your focus should be on something bigger and greater than you are.

If, at the end of your life, there are trophies and money and world acclaim you may be described as successful. If you leave something greater than you are that carries on, you may be described as significant.

Make today a significant one.

19

Suck it Up and Move Forward

One of the nagging questions that appear in the mind of those who consider new business or personal goals is, "Am I ready to jump in, or have I waited until the window of opportunity is gone and I'm now too late?"

I've noted that many people never begin a new business venture, risk new personal relationships, fail to reach out for spiritual growth, or other desirable goals, because they are overcome with fear.

Fear, like the fear of failure, success and the unknown, prevents many people from ever realizing their dreams. They wake up one day and understand they've exhausted their options and have little time left with which to realize those dreams. But you can avoid this dilemma if you take action.

Fear of Failure

I was 20 years old when I began investing in my own businesses. Some of my close friends and co-workers thought I had gone crazy. They knew I didn't have any money and they thought I was too young. As I aged and enjoyed a level of success, there were still people who laughed at me and told me I was crazy. I have learned over the years there is no shortage of "experts." Everybody has an opinion, and everyone has a horror story of a friend going broke. Interestingly, the most vocal negative voices seem to be those who have never done anything on their own.

If you want to be triumphant in your life goals, rule number one is very simple: don't hang around with negative thinkers. They will fill your heads with "what ifs." What if you can't make a monthly payment? What if the economy falls flat? What if you lose all your money? What if you get sued? What if you can't do this or that?? The "what ifs" are endless and can make you very nervous.

When I purchased my first property I didn't know a lot about real estate investing. In the late 60's I read William Nickerson's classic work, ***How I Turned $1,000 Into A $1,000,000***. From that book, I learned about a formula that made sense to me and I latched onto the promise of real estate riches. I re-read the book, took notes, and jumped in. I had reduced my risk some by getting a little education before I took the dive. Maybe I wasn't old enough to know better, but I had no fear of failure. Nickerson had done it so I knew that I could do it, too. It was as simple as that.

My wife and I purchased a building lot in Santa Rosa, California for $5,000 with no money down. Then, we borrowed a total of $19,000 to pay off the lot and build our first house - also with no money down. We lived in it a year and then sold it for $36,000. After deducting a 6% real estate fee, we netted about $14,840 -twice what I had earned in my construction job and with far less effort because I hired people to build most of the house. It seemed to me to be a great way to make a living.

I could have listened to those who thought I was getting in over my head. I could have decided that I was too young - just like some of them said. I could have been wrapped in fear of failure

- but I wasn't. In my mind there was no reason not to take the risk. I had nothing to lose.

Fear of Success

Why do people fear success? I think there is something in their past that they are dealing with. Whatever the reason, some people feel undeserving of success. They are continually subconsciously sabotaging their dreams, hopes, and desires. They have a recurring negative mental image that takes a place of priority in their thinking - what I call negative self talk. They think they're not worthy or deserving of a good life. And they know it's true because they tell themselves this in countless different ways.

You have to replace the negative self talk with positive affirmations. I want your positive affirmations to become a self fulfilling prophesy. I want you to understand there's more out there. I want you to capture and enjoy success. I want you to experience greater accomplishments and fulfill your God-given potential.

I understand that life is not easy and there are many crushing disappointments. But I also passionately believe that it is possible to come to terms with your past and move forward. A negative life does not have to continue. In fact you can bring it to an end right this second by changing your thought process from "I can't" to "I can!"

Fear of the Unknown

When I was 14 years old I lived near a bridge that crossed the Russian River. The boys in our town liked to jump from the bridge into the river and I longed to do the same but the thought terrified me. Even though no one seemed to be getting hurt, I was still scared.

One day I made up my mind I was going to do it. I remember that first jump as though it was yesterday. I still feel the fear swelling up inside me. I still feel the wind slapping my face while falling through mid air. I can feel the cool water as my feet broke the surface and I plummeted into the depths of the water, my knees buckling when I hit the river bottom. Gasping for air as my head cleared the surface of the water, I had a feeling of success! I had done it. I had proven myself to my peers. In the process I had overcome my fear.

After my successful jump it was much easier the second time. It got easier with each additional jump and eventually there was no fear at all associated with jumping.

To a large degree, we overcome fears with information. You get information by reading books, having a mentor, taking a class, purchasing a course, attending a boot camp, networking with like minded people and through experience. What is keeping you from jumping in your new venture, relationship or growth?

Here's what you do to overcome your fears and get started:

> 1. If you fear failure, get some information and take action today. It's the only way to gain power over your fear of failure.

> 2. If you fear success, define what it is that you want to accomplish and engage in positive self talk and affirmations. Changing your mindset will come much easier if you do this.

> 3. If you fear the unknown, jump in anyway. The water's fine out here! Jump in and enjoy the exhilaration of success.

> Now, go make it a great day.

20

Overcoming the Negative 101

Negative thinking will cripple your spirit and curtail your creativity. It also generates a black cloud that overshadows your life and makes you cynical.

Although I'm an unusually positive and optimistic person, I must confess in the interest of transparency, there are times I have negative thoughts and sometimes those thoughts lead me to negative emotional responses as well.

Let me share some tips that help me break the negative thought processes that can so easily spiral out of control.

1. Negative thinkers are usually complainers. As a personal coach, I will tell you that if you are going to be a complainer, it would be better if you do nothing.

    When you recognize you are complaining, immediately stop and right away look for something positive to say. You can only think one thought at a time, so spend more time on the positive and you will have a life transformation.

There are times we get so caught up with all the bad stuff going on that we forget to look for, and appreciate, the good. After you finish reading this, make a written list of the positives in your life and the encouraging things that happened today no matter how diminutive.

2.   Everything you say negative about yourself is a mental suggestion that leads you to be comfortable with a lesser you. I have a psychologist friend who suggests that negative self talk is really a form of self hypnosis with which you sabotage your life, success, and happiness.

If you find yourself thinking, "Boy, I'm sure dumb," stop and immediately recognize your error. Instead, rephrase it using positive self-talk. For example, "That's not like me. I'm very capable. Next time I will do it differently." According to my friend, this is also a form of self hypnosis. But this approach is much more positive for you and attaining your goals.

3.   If you want to find solutions for your problems, a negative attitude is self defeating. You will not find them by looking for someone (or something) to blame because that doesn't really address the real problem, which most of the time is you.

People will be naturally drawn to you if you take personal responsibility for your situation(s) and have a positive outlook on trials and challenges. Determine to be an inspiration to the people around you.

4.   We all have heard the saying, "Birds of a feather flock together." That principle is true of people with similar

mindsets. Negative thinkers tend to attract more of the same because they feed off each other. Conversely, positive thinkers attract people of a similar mindset. Which do you attract? For which would you prefer to be a magnet?

My challenge to you is very simple. Realize that your thoughts don't own you – you are in charge of what you think. It may take real work on your part, but you will benefit and be in a better position to enjoy success in your business, relationships, and spiritual life when you replace your negative words with positive ones. As a bonus, your life will be enriched because you will be drawn to positive and uplifting people.

Now, go make it a great day.

Life is an opportunity, benefit from it.
Life is beauty, admire it.
Life is bliss, taste it.
Life is a dream, realize it.
Life is a challenge, meet it.
Life is a duty, complete it.
Life is a game, play it.
Life is a promise, fulfill it.
Life is sorrow, overcome it.
Life is a song, sing it.
Life is a struggle, accept it.
Life is a tragedy, confront it.
Life is an adventure, dare it.
Life is luck, make it.
Life is too precious, do not destroy it.
Life is life, fight for it.

Mother Teresa

21

Influence of a System

The difference between those with goals and those who achieve them is very simple. Success comes to those who have a system they utilize to help them arrive at the desired destination.

A system is the procedure or process employed in order to achieve a defined objective. The reason 90 - 95% of new businesses fail is the lack of systems used by new business owners. Conversely, an explanation for such a high rate of success (more than 90%) among various franchise opportunities is the utilization of proven systems.

When I was 24 years old I decided I would become a general contractor. It struck me as an easy way to make money. My mindset was, *if they can do, I can do it.* What I failed to realize, however, was that to be a successful general contractor I needed more than the ability to build a wall or pour a foundation.

I was in for a real education.

My first project as a licensed general contractor was a financial disaster. I worked hard for three or four months, but I actually earned very little money for my hard work when the house sold.

As a result, I explored the reasons why some builders succeeded and others didn't. The common denominator was that those with a reproducible system were much more successful than those who just built a house hoping to sell it at some point.

If you want to succeed in your business venture, you must develop and use systems. You need procedures that make easy work for your marketing outreach, sales process, bookkeeping and accounting chores, customer follow up efforts, purchasing requirements, etc.

I know this approach is boring to many whom start a new business. But, you must be confident that if you do "A" the result will be "B." Take the guess work out of the equation and enjoy the knowledge of a successful outcome before you make an effort or spend your money.

As a bonus, when you develop systems, you increase the value of the business and you have something you can market and sell. Savvy business buyers will pay more for your company when you have proven systems with reproducible results.

Reproducible systems will allow you to exponentially grow your business. If you are so inclined, you can have multiple locations (regional or national), license your business name to others, develop a franchise, or explore other options.

Start today working on developing, or streamlining, your business systems.

Now, go make it a awe-inspiring day.

22

Positive Expectancy

"It all begins with a dream. A dream is like a seed that when watered and nourished grows into a grand experience or noble cause. If you want to see tomorrow, dream. A dream is a glimpse into the future." I wrote those words in my book, "My New Reality Journal."

It's important to dream. God has given you the ability to do great things regardless of the challenges. And success or failure is up to you.

As you know by now, I grew up with a speech impediment. As difficult as it was to endure, I determined not to let it, or people's reaction to it, stand in the way of my dreams. I decided those who poked fun or ridiculed me were not in charge of my life.

The story is not that I had a speech problem. The story is I had a speech problem, so what! The fact is, all of us have a "handicap." Some handicaps are visible, but the most destructive ones are those that are not visible – the mental stumbling blocks that can lead to mediocrity and failure.

So what if you were born into poverty?
So what if your dad left when you were a baby?
So what if everybody thinks you're not too bright?
So what if you think you look funny (or sound funny like I did)?
So what if you didn't go to college?
So what if you've faced some real life-changing tragedy?

So what?

You still have the choice between success and failure and it depends to a large degree on your mindset. You are unique, God made only one of you. You have something important to offer and share with the rest of us.

Oprah Winfrey wrote in O Magazine, *"I've come to believe that each of us has a personal calling that's as unique as a fingerprint - and that the best way to succeed is to discover what you love and then find a way to offer it to others in the form of service, working hard, and also allowing the energy of the universe to lead you."*

That's enormous advice! The key mindset is a *positive expectancy*. The important thing is the journey you take.

Live life on purpose, not by chance and never fear failure. Work hard, and smart, to change your reality by enlarging your dreams. I'm confident you'll find the process a worthwhile and exciting challenge.

Don't limit your possibilities by dreaming small. Warmly embrace huge dreams.

Now, go dream and dream BIG.

23

Self Talk –

No, You're Not Nuts

I write a lot about changing our current mindset to a more robust and accommodating one. To a large degree, how we talk to ourselves will determine success or failure in our business endeavors, personal relationships and spiritual growth.

In our minds we categorize and classify every situation we face. We mentally interpret and characterize a tone of voice, words spoken, our reaction to events, and much, much more. This internal voice is what is referred to as self talk.

Far from being a sign of senility or having a screw loose, talking to oneself can be healthy and productive. If used correctly, it can be a tremendous tool in changing our mindset and outlook on life.

Things go wrong all the time. Sometimes expectations are hard to meet. We make mistakes and bad choices every day. How do those errors and missteps make you feel? It's really up to you.

Those who are successful view the above with positive self talk. Instead of saying to themselves, "I sure am dumb! I'll always be a failure" (reinforcing the mental thoughts that you are, in your mind, a failure) they turn the negative into a positive and their self talk is more representative of, "You know, that wasn't like me. I will choose better next time – I know I can do better" (reinforcing a positive mental image that allows you to face the day with anticipation).

In 1970 I learned the importance of positive self talk. I was twenty years old and took a sales training course so I could "get rich" selling an expensive item door-to-door.

You have already read that I had a terrible speech impediment, and I think one thing that helped me overcome it, at least in part, was the positive affirmations I repeated daily. When thrown a curve, I adjusted by restating the challenge in a positive way.

The mental self talk you cultivate molds your personality. It controls what people see in your life and hear in your speech – not to mention your own success or failure. Positively controlling mental self talk will pay off in spades. "I could never do this," becomes, "I know I can do this – that's the way I am. I'm very capable" The result is you become an even greater achiever than you are now.

Embrace positive self talk and make it a superb day.

24

Buck UP -Take Personal Responsibility

There's no magic pill that will make you happy or successful. The simple fact is you have to face your fears and go in the direction of your choice. If your goal is to succeed in your family life, business dealings, spiritual growth or social circles, you must take the bull by the horns and address those areas – and it begins by taking personal responsibilities for your choices and actions.

Our culture no longer believes in taking personal responsibility. People are eager to place blame elsewhere. For example, if you made a bad decision in a real estate investment, it had to be the fault of the sales person, developer, or someone else close to the transaction. If you lost money in the stock market, it has to be the broker's fault or the bad advice from Uncle Harry.

If your personal life is in shambles, of course the cause is the spouse you married or your family of origin. The causes of your failures seem to belong to everyone but whom really is at fault. That would be you.

Here's how you unlock to the door to enjoying the freedom of success in all areas of your life. Before you develop positive, self-affirming, self-talk scripts to enhance your personal development and growth:

1. Acknowledge that you are solely responsible for the choices.

2. Accept that you are responsible for what you choose to feel or think.

3. Accept that you choose the direction for your life.

4. Accept that you cannot blame others for the choices you have made.

5. Tear down the facade of defense or rationale for why others are responsible for who you are or what has happened to you.

6. Embrace the belief that you are responsible for determining who you are.

7. Point the finger of responsibility back to yourself when you discuss the consequences of your actions.

8. Take an honest inventory of your strengths, abilities, talents, virtues and positive points.

9. Let go of blame and anger toward those in your past who did the best they could, given the limitations of their knowledge, background and awareness.

10. Let go of your anger, hostility, pessimism and depression over past hurts, pains, abuse, mistreatment and misdirection.

I know from personal experience that it's easy to name all the things that rendered you incapable of reaching your goals, but it's a good deal more gratifying to tell others how the same things didn't stop you and to describe the brilliance with which you met each challenge (not to mention how you were inspired to succeed).

Successful people don't place blame or make excuses - because they don't have to. There is almost nothing you can't plow through or work around.

From this day forward, choose to take responsibility for your own actions and choices. Find the power in taking personal responsibility and you will be free to live a much fuller and happier life. It's amazing how liberating it is to rid yourself of the negative energy associated with the blame game.

Now, go make it a great day.

Do one thing every day

that scares you.
Eleanor Roosevelt

25

How to Rev Up Your Engine

I often ask my new protégées, "How much income do you want?" It's not uncommon for them to respond with $100,000 a year. To which I routinely ask, "You don't really believe you can make that much, do you?" The answer, more often than not, is, "Well, no, not really."

Will those that believe in their heart they can only earn $30,000 a year consistently earn $100,000? No! Henry Ford said it well when he said, *"Whether you think you can or whether you think you can't, you're right."*

This principle is not limited to money or business success. It's applicable across the board of human experience. We feel comfortable only when we perform or live within our belief system.

Auto-suggestion is simply a way to reprogram your thoughts. If you are religious or spiritual, you might call it meditation. For example, I'm a Christian so I meditate on Scripture that on which reinforces where I believe God would have me focus. For example, "I can do all things through Christ who gives me strength." Or, "Ask and it shall be given to you, seek and you will find, knock and it will be opened to you." How about, "If there be any virtue, if there be any praise . . . think on these things."

The above, and many other Scriptures, addresses positive reinforcement on what I wish to focus. Positively worded daily scripts (auto-suggestions) will re-program your mind to accept a new reality about yourself. Your subconscious will faithfully draw into your mind that which is fed into it by what you think.

If you think things like, "I am not creative," "I am not happy," "I am poor," "I am unhealthy," you are training yourself to feel comfortable with this reality. Here's the bottom line: Whatever you think, you are. Richard Bach suggests that if you "argue for your limitations ... sure enough, they're yours."

If you want to create the life you desire, or live your life with specific purpose, fill your mind with statements (or scripture, or prayer, or . . .) which reinforce and assemble the new reality. The flip side of Bach's statement is just as telling. If you argue for your excellence [with auto-suggestion], that is yours as well.

You have the power to use positive affirmations to re-direct your mind. Think about it! You have the power to set a new course for your life. The question is, will you?

Make it a great day and a great new reality.

26

Big Goals and Baby Steps

Each December, like many others before, millions of people will gear up for their New Year's resolutions. It's a time of reflection on the events of the past year and plans to improve the results for the next.

Many people want improvement because they're not happy with the way things are. I believe there are two reasons for this. Some have not created a concrete picture of how they want their lives to be different, nor do they have any idea of which direction they're going.

As a result, many people fall short and abandon their goals within few weeks. I don't think the problem in discarding goals lies with the goals themselves – it's found in a lack of commitment and definite planning.

As it relates to your new goals for the coming year, here's what I suggest:

1. Sit down with a new yellow pad. That blank tablet is your future. Notice that there's no writing on it which

means no one has defined your future. Now, write down what you want to accomplish in the next five years in your businesses, spiritual growth, personal life, and personal relationships. Please dream big, even if it sounds to you too big or too silly, and be specific. Rather than stating "I want to get rich," state, "I will net $1,000,000 by December 20, 2015." Then, create a <u>real heart felt commitment</u> to it. Without a commitment you are only hoping.

2. Establish how you will reach your goals. For example, if your goal is financial and you are in widget sales, state, in writing, that you will realize your goal by selling 10,000 widgets.

3. Breakdown your goals into more manageable segments. First, define your five year plan and what you will accomplish in the first year. The yearly goal breaks down into monthly, and then weekly goals. If you have to sell 10,000 widgets in five years to reach your goal, you may determine that you need to sell 2,000 widgets each year. That equates to 167 (rounded up) per month, or 38.5 per week.

4. Now, identify the daily activity you will need to do if you are to accomplish your weekly goal of widgets. You should find that the daily activity and effort needed by you is a very minor thing in terms of time and effort. The important thing is to **do the daily activity**.

5. Since we consistently perform within our belief systems (mind set), many times we need to change those. To help you make your goals more attainable, prepare and read written affirmations that inspire a new mindset (like: "Of course I sell 2,000 widgets each year. That's what I do. I consistently perform at that level. I actually feel most comfortable and relaxed there).

You will comfortably work at the new level of performance because your belief system changes and tells you that it's "normal" for you to perform at that (new) level. It's much like the thermostat for your heating system. When you set the comfort level for 70 degrees, the furnace automatically turns off at 70 degrees. If you want to function at a higher level, raise the comfort level of your thinking by changing the setting on your mental thermostat.

When you take action and do the daily activities - taking first one baby step at a time - you can accomplish enormous things. You are only limited by your imagination and mindset. Mark Twain wrote: "Loyalty to a petrified opinion never yet broke a chain or freed a human soul."

My challenge to you is to break the chain of the belief system (Twain's "petrified opinion") that keeps you in your current mindset comfort zone so that you can enjoy the freedom that comes with a new reality.

Make it a profitable day.

Life is what happens to you

While you're busy making other plans.
John Lennon

27

Liberation

In my experience there is at least one observation worth mentioning: Most people are limited by their own thinking and mindset. Regardless of your own personal disillusionment, frustration or mistreatment, you have the ability to break free and soar with eagles. You "have the key." No! You **_are_** the key.

All too often, thoughts passing through your mind are accepted without judgment or attention given to the final result of that thinking. But there are always consequences, good or bad, in what you think.

Most people are not aware that they are thinking – it's like an automated routine. But your mind is like a sponge that will take in whatever you invite in. If you allow your mind to behave without constraint, you lose freedom. "Magic" occurs when you control your thinking and then refuse to believe everything that goes through your mind.

For example, you think, "I'm poor and I'll always be poor." That statement is false, but it will have a negative effect on you if you fail to correct it. Most of us in America define "poor" as not having the latest and the greatest HDTV set. By world standards, even those among us with the least, are rich. Poor is when you don't have shelter or something to eat.

If your thought is negative, it may cause you a great deal of trouble. When you think you are poor (or ugly, or disadvantaged, or unloved, etc.), control it by restating it in different terms. Say something like this: My desire is to do better and have more. If I will do _____, I will achieve my goal."

When someone directs hurtful words to you, are they true? One writer asks: "Most people think and believe that their thoughts originate from them, but have they ever stopped and considered whether their thoughts, desires, likes and dislikes are really theirs? Maybe they have come from the outside, and they have unconsciously accepted them as their own? If there is no filter to process the thoughts that enter the mind, there is no freedom. Then all actions are like the actions of a puppet on a string, though no one will admit it."

What follows is a personal story I want you to consider. It's a story that many can relate to. The result may surprise you and give confidence that you can to have a better life – however you define "better."

As you have already read, I was the object of much ridicule and hurtful words growing up. I was mimicked, laughed at, and physically accosted. As a teenager, I decided that those who did and said those things were not in charge of my life and they would not negatively impact it.

In fact, the opposite was true. I dreamed of a day when I would drive into town in my new Cadillac Eldorado, THE status symbol of the day, and have the former high school football star pump my gas (although there is nothing wrong with pumping gas for a living). I actually visualized that scene. I used the hurtful things done to me as stepping stones to success.

Why allow outside influences determine <u>your</u> success or failure? You settle on those things you choose to believe. Break free! If you want to be the captain of your ship, you set the rules for what you'll believe and accept as true.

I want to challenge you into action. Find power in breaking free. I want you to use all the good things you've enjoyed, and bad influences you've endured, as positive building blocks. It's your choice. What will you do?

Make it a liberating day.

Don Loyd

We make a living by what we get,

we make a life by what we give.

Winston Churchill

28

How to Gain Peace of Mind

In counseling with individuals, I've observed that most want to be happy and be able to forget their problems, worries and troubles. They are eager to discover an inner calmness and enjoy the freedom that comes from controlling their negative, worrying thoughts so they can sleep peacefully at night. They want peace of mind.

To make any progress in this arena you have to first describe what peace of mind is. Here's my suggestion: Peace of mind is really an inner calmness resulting in a feeling of inner tranquility. When that is achieved, you discover a freedom that comes as worries collapse and stress is relieved.

I'll share with you seven steps I use to find power in peace of mind. Perhaps my experience in dealing with stress will assist you in your quest to find peace of mind so you can sleep at night, too.

1. Recognize that stress, strain, fear, and all that goes with those, is a normal, human experience – but they are controllable if you execute power over them. Take personal responsibility for your choices and learn from

situations that surround you. In many cases, the choices you make, and the actions you take, are the basis for your stress and strain.

2. Believe that you can create a new confidence by changing your mindset. Your job is to fashion a habit of controlling your thought processes by using positive affirmations and self talk. Fortunately, this is in your control.

3. Honestly evaluate your strengths and weaknesses and accept what you cannot change. When you face circumstances out of your control, just do the best you can and move forward. Create a mastermind group to help fill in the areas in which you are weak and supply positive support.

4. It's not always possible to change all the inconveniences and irritations we face very day. If it's within your power to change them, do so. But if you cannot change them, learn how to willingly accept those as part of living and move forward. Also, reduce the amount of time you read a newspaper or watch television news stories. If you aren't careful, they will keep you stirred up and stressed out.

5. Stay away from negative people and negative conversations which will only amplify your stress and feeling of vulnerability. This is another area we can control. So, surround yourself with positive minded people.

6. When someone does something awful or unpleasant to you, quickly deal with the incident as positively as possible and let it go. Since you can only think of one thing at a time, remember if you are holding a grudge, that person to whom your bitterness is focused is

controlling you. Learn lessons from the past, but bring to an end ruminating the past and focus on the present and future.

7. Don't take everything personally. Most of the things said by others are spoken in moments of passion, fear, hate, or without thought. When someone spouts off, or acts indifferently, they are saying more about themselves than they are you. The result of embracing this principle is learning how to stay detached as you practice patience and tolerance.

Finally, remember that you are in control. The important issue is how you address those things in your control. I encourage you to make the most of what you have and not be fretful about what you think is missing. Ultimately, peace of mind and the resulting external peace will come to those who make use of these seven steps.

Now, take action and have a good night sleep.

He is a wise man who does not grieve for

the things which he has not,

but rejoices for those which he has.
Epictetus

29

In Search of Happiness

Happiness is an elusive, fleeting thing, but everyone is looking for it. It's hard to get your arms around it because it has to do with your mindset, and it's almost always dependent upon other people or events.

If you allow people or events to influence how you feel, you lose control and give permission to be their slaves in the process of losing your freedom. People and events, then, control you. How does that make you feel?

Daily life can be made happier. But, true contented happiness is not something that is contingent upon other people or the way the proverbial cards are dealt.

Finding true happiness will really bring power into your life because you're unselfishly serving others. Happiness begins to occur when you get the focus off of self.

Here are some tips on finding what almost everyone is looking for.

1. Serve. Find a place where you can give to others. As long as your goal is feeding yourself and your ego, happiness will be just around the next corner. I've spent most of my life giving, and it is great.

2. Try your best to look on the bright side of events. Even in bad situations, there are good things that can take root. I try to appreciate the positive of every situation.

3. Do you have problems? No, you have opportunities to find solutions. Finding solutions is like living life on a treasure hunt. It can be exciting and exhilarating. So, enjoy the journey.

4. Learn to laugh. A wise man once wrote: "Laughter is good medicine." Laughter will lighten your load and make the day much more pleasant and approachable.

5. Schedule time each day to read inspirational material. Read about people being successful or overcoming obstacles. I've overcome obstacles as have many of my friends. It's thrilling to read about and spend time with people who successfully swam against the current.

6. Guard your thoughts. When you find yourself thinking negatively, turn it around into a positive experience. I've said for years, even though it's trite, that if I get served a lemon, I will do my best to sell lemonade.

7. Rather than focusing on what you think is missing in your life, look at what you do have and how you are blessed. You have accomplished a lot. Rejoice on those things. If you missed your goal today, there's always tomorrow to make adjustments.

8. Celebrate your successes and those of others. Also, look for opportunities to associate with people who are generally successful and happy. The pleasure of "happiness" is infectious.

9. Smile more often. Mother Teresa said, "Every time you smile at someone, it is an action of love, a gift to that person, a beautiful thing." The physical act of smiling will make you more positive and feel better.

Now, go make it a great day.

I have a simple philosophy:

Fill what's empty.

Empty what's full.

Scratch where it itches.

Alice Roosevelt Longworth

30

Giving Back

One virtue that separates the "haves" from the "have not's" is the ability to give one's time and money. If all we do is take from others (could be the government, our parents, our family, our friends, etc.), we suffer the same fate as the Dead Sea in the Middle East. There, there is no outlet for the water that feeds that lake so all activity is focused in feeding it. The consequence is, nothing lives in the Dead Sea – it's dead. It's so full of stuff, you can't even sink there!!

Giving, rather than taking, frees us to live a more contented, fulfilled and productive life. For example, a mountain brook is a place where life and abundance thrive. As that stream twists and falls toward the river or ocean, there is fresh, new life everywhere. The stream feeds trees, grasses, wild flowers, wild life and more. It's a true blessing to everything within its reach.

Which would you rather be? Would you rather be like a bubbling, life giving stream, or a stagnate body of water that breads death?

Volunteering for community service is one way to give back. I have given back to my community for most of my adult life.

Among the many opportunities I took advantage of, I volunteered for several years serving on the counseling staff at our local hospital. I've been at the bedside of several people who died, then counseled the bereaved family. Other times I was there to visit those who simply needed someone to drop by and leave a kind word.

The things I did were not news worthy or of major importance in terms of public relations. But over the years I've learned that getting involved in giving back does have several positive effects for us that I want you to consider.

1.   What you sow, you reap. Some will call this Karma. Whatever you want to call it, when you do good things, good things come back to you. When you maintain a positive flow outward (and get the focus off of self), there will always be a return toward you. In my experience, the inward flow is greater than the outward flow.

2.   Networking opportunities results, too. When you are in the community, people see you and you have a great impact on people you may have never met had you not volunteered. If you are unemployed, volunteering for community service will help you in many ways. First, it keeps your mind active and gets you out of the house. Second, it puts you in front of more employment opportunities. You never know who you will meet.

3.   Volunteering can help give you perspective. You may find that many others are worse off than you are, giving you a chance to be thankful for what you have – always a worthy thing. You begin to more clearly understand what truly matters in life and helps you build a stronger foundation on which to personally grow.

4. You learn new skills and have greater understanding. Had I not volunteered for the hospital counseling staff, I would have missed out on a lot of solid learning experiences which helped me develop into the person I am. I think you can learn to understand people better, too, when you are introduced to people outside your comfort zone.

5. It "feels" good to help others and give back. Believe it when I say that you will get a "warm and fuzzy" thing going on when you give. For me, giving helped make since of life. It exemplified a purpose and made me feel needed. Besides, it cleared my mind so I could more easily focus on my business interests.

6. People will remember your generosity. How do you want to be remembered? What you do with your time and treasure will be remembered after you are gone.

Have you ever noticed that the most miserable people are those who think only of themselves? There is much more to life than taking. Learn to give and you will be introduced to a full life. Get involved and give. Become that sparkling, bubbling mountain stream that blesses everything in its path.

Now, it's up to you. Create a wonderful giving back kind of day.

Be glad of life because it gives you the

chance to love and to work and to play

and to look up at the stars.
Henry Van Dyke

31

Supremacy in Simply Doing

Like you, I've felt like quitting. I understand the feeling of helplessness and loneliness when my business weathers the pinch of the economy, or my personal life is barren of meaningful relationships. But I know in my heart that quitting means I've failed.

Success, while meaning different things to different people, is indicative of persistence – a never say die attitude. You set a goal, create plan to achieve the goal, and do the daily activity needed to reach the destination.

You try, and try, and try! You try with your personal relationships, career, business interests and the like.

The word "try" means you are "attempting" or "enduring." But the truth is, you cannot succeed until you stop "trying" and simply do it. I suggest that if all you do is "attempt," or "endure," you may never succeed in anything other than "attempting" or "enduring."

Don't try to be a success! Be a success. But here's the hard part - that involves a change in mindset. Instead of, "Oh, woe is me!" it emerges into, "Oh YEA, is me." Not a "look at me cause I'm so great" attitude, but an "I've got a purpose" lifestyle.

There is good and bad in almost every situation. Train yourself to see the good. Think on good, and honorable, and pure things. Here's what I want you to do:

1.   Look at each new day with positive expectancy. Sure, some things will go wrong. But that's okay – it's a part of life.

2.   Don't focus so much on what you want and when you want it. Look for ways that you can help others. A totally self-focused life is truly a shallow and empty way to live.

3.   Look for daily blessings and positive experiences you can share with others. There are hurting people who need your positive input.

4.   Just simply go for it and "*gitter*" done.

5.   Be a mentor to someone else. Bring them along for a great ride, too. Share what you know and have experienced.

Do you want to be a success? Fine – I'm on your side! Stop trying and find the power in simply doing it.

Now, go make it a successful day.

32

Renewal ASAP

Have you ever felt like you're burning the candle at both ends? Are you so busy that you don't know how much longer you can endure the stress? Let's face it, you are burned out!

Burnout is a common complaint. In today's economic climate, individuals are putting out one fire after another and running from here to there at a hurried tempo.

If you are physically and emotionally exhausted because of prolonged stress and frustration, likely you have joined the growing number of burnout fatalities. The foundational problem is that you have failed to plan a balanced life.

You are like the hot tub that never receives ph balance or the proper chemicals to retard the growth of organisms. You keep circulating, you look productive, and you may even feel nice and warm. But the fact is, you are unbalanced and breeding disease and discomfort to those around you – not to mention yourself.

How do you know when you are facing burnout? Here are some hints:

You're irritable to those around you
You're negative when you were once very positive
You have strained personal relationships
Maybe you're just "plain-ole-tired" most of the time
You're not able to rest
You withdraw from personal interaction with others

Sound familiar?

If you want to enjoy a more balanced life, I have a few suggestions.

1. Realize that you are a threefold-being. Exercise, rest (addressed in point 3) and eat right in order to keep your physical body working properly. You have a mind that needs time to refresh; so, budget the time to feed and exercise it with good thoughts and reading material. You have a spiritual side you need to address as well. Feed it, too (if you need some help here, contact me and I will offer suggestions).

2. Learn to delegate tasks. None of us can be all or do all. Delegation will result in more achievement with less strain and personal focus.

3. Get some rest. In our culture we wrestle with this issue. You may have to pencil in your calendar a time for rest and recreation. John Lubbock, an English Biologist at the turn of the 20th Century wrote:

    "Rest is not idleness, and to lie sometimes on the grass under the trees on a summer's day, listening to the murmur of water, or watching the clouds float across the sky, is by no means a waste of time"

4. Nurture good, positive relationships. One thing I have recently come to realize in a very real way is that we are created to be with others. We need the input, council and companionship from people who will offer positive support.

5. Learn to laugh. King Solomon, a recognized expert on personal responsibility, informs his readers to laugh. He calls it good medicine. In fact, there is clinical evidence to support the idea that laughter is good for your brain and good for your blood vessels. In other words, it's healthy to laugh.

Now is a good time to take personal responsibility and recognize that you are burnt out because of choices you have made and you need a time of refreshing. Acknowledge that some changes are needed, define what those changes are, formulate a plan to embrace those changes, and create the time for renewal. You will not regret it.

For if there is a sin against life, it

consists perhaps not so much in

despairing of life as in hoping for

another life and in eluding the

implacable grandeur of this life.
Albert Camus

33

In Search of Baby Steps

The great philosopher and basketball star, Shaquille O'Neal said, *"Excellence is not a singular act, but a habit. You are what you repeatedly do."*

Whether or not the Shaq is a great philosopher, I will leave up to you. But, he is right on point in this quote. More precisely, taking forward strides in your business, relationships, family and spiritual growth is not a matter of taking huge, giant steps in one single bound. It's a matter of focusing on taking little baby steps each day.

Success is about doing the small things repeatedly until those actions and attitudes become second nature. It's like the Egyptians building the Pyramids. The repetitive nature of cutting, transporting and placing the stones, one stone at time, resulted in one of the great wonders of the ancient world.

When you take one small forward step at a time, you will soon realize that you've had a successful day. Then, when repeated, you have had a successful week. And believe it or not, if you have enough successful weeks, you are enjoying a successful year. Finally, you have acquired the habit of success as you constantly whittle away at the small things.

The interesting thing about taking little steps is that each day you are adding "stones" which lay the foundation for future large success. Success boils down to just doing all that you can today!

 My advice and practice is: Don't worry about tomorrow - it will take care of itself. And many of your imaginary obstacles will never materialize anyway.

When you just focus on the small things today, you are not overworked and you don't have to rush around bouncing from pillar to post. Earl Nightingale supports the idea like this: "*It's not the number of things you do, but the quality, the efficiency of each separate action, that counts.*"

There is tremendous power that comes from forming good habits. In the early 80s I was hired by National Bank of Alaska to originate home loans. Before they allowed me to generate business, I had to work as a loan processor for three months. Management wanted me to learn the basics of loan processing, the little repetitive things, so that I would be a better prepared loan officer.

I must admit that I didn't like being a loan processor and I couldn't wait to get out of that job. But it did teach me the importance of the little things. Once I hit the streets originating loans, my loan packages were complete and easy to process. It was the little things, done over and over again, that made the difference.

If you want to enjoy success, I offer you this:

1. Don't get impatient and accept a life of mediocrity. The choice is yours, so choose excellence.

2. Set your sight on the goal of your daily activity (the little things that when stacked on each other will help you realize your ultimate goal). Focus on the important tasks.

3. As you go about your day, there will be many disruptions and distractions that will tempt you to get off target. You are in control! Do not allow distractions to dictate your activities.

4. Stay in focused motion. There will be good days and not-so-good days. Enjoy the good ones, learn lessons from the bad ones, and move forward, keeping your eye on the target.

5. As you form good habits, both physical and mental, your load becomes lighter and your successes cultivate more success.

6. It's important that you share your success with at least one other person. Be a mentor to someone by sharing what you know and have experienced. If you will, your life becomes more meaningful and has greater purpose.

Now, go make it a successful day.

God asks no man whether he will accept

life. That is not the choice. You must

take it. The only question is how.

Henry Ward Beecher

34

Nothing Better Than Hope

When you think about achieving goals, regardless of their nature, one mental condition that unites them is hope. Hope is not positive thinking, a process used to cure pessimism. It's not wishing something false were true.

Hope is assurance in a positive outcome. As such, those who have hope embrace some kind of belief system. Hope originates from within us predicated on experience, personal knowledge and faith in our underlying authority source.

I've noticed that those with hope can be much more forward thinking and optimistic in their view of the events of any given day. Even when momentarily taken aback, they readjust and move forward. For them, hope is something alive and authentic.

Barbara Kingsolver suggests that it's something that lives inside us. She declared: "The very least you can do in your life is to figure out what you hope for. And the most you can do is live inside that hope. Not admire it from a distance but live right in it, under its roof."

If you want the peace of mind that can come with success, embrace hope and make it an important part of your life. Live in hope and make it a reality.

Having hope in some respects is similar to the person who sees the glass half full rather than half empty. The difference is, those with hope look forward with expectation seeing the half full glass topped off. Based on their experience, knowledge and belief system, they look forward to that overflowing glass – even if it takes years to fill.

During the Great Depression and the 1930s Dust Bowl, millions of Americans looked forward in hope as they loaded up the Model T and headed for California (or remained in their homes to wait for a better day). One hymn they sang and cherished talked about a hope for tomorrow. It says in part:

> *Soft as the voice of an angel,*
> *Breathing a lesson unheard,*
> *Hope with a gentle persuasion*
> *Whispers her comforting word:*
> *Wait till the darkness is over,*
> *Wait till the tempest is done,*
> *Hope for the sunshine tomorrow,*
> *After the shower is gone.*
> *Whispering hope, oh, how welcome thy voice,*
> *Making my heart in its sorrow rejoice.*

Hope allows for rejoicing in troublesome times. It keeps us on an even keel.

In 2010 relocated to Portland, Oregon. I have hope that the rain will stop and I will see the sun again and feel it's warmth.

My experience tells me that after rain and more rain, Portlanders will take pleasure in sunshine. My knowledge supports the idea that as the world rotates, more favorable weather cycles will bring sunshine. My belief system sustains the idea (even the fact) that, unless someone introduces some kind of outside event that negates Mother Nature, I will see the sun soon and feel warm again.

If you have hope, find something about which you can celebrate. Just remember that there are millions of people on this earth that would trade places with you in a heartbeat.

"There is no medicine like hope, no incentive so great, and no tonic so powerful as expectation of something tomorrow."

Orison Swett Marden

I hope you enjoy a hope filled day. Make it so.

Life is like a ten-speed bicycle.

Most of us have gears we never use.

Charles Schulz

35

Credibility – A Key to Success

Credibility is one cornerstone to success. Without it, you will not go far in your business. Earlier, I wrote about the importance of systems as it relates to success. Here I want to address credibility.

Credibility means people believe you, and trust you to the extent that it is worthy of belief. Once you have the confidence of your client or prospective client, they are willing to do business with you.

If you are new to your industry, or a low performer, define your niche market and become an expert in it. Sounds easy enough, but in reality it's a little more difficult. I will share with you some things I have done to help create this thing referred to as credibility.

If you believe your experience or knowledge is not yet fully developed, speak to those who know less than you do. If you're the "expert," most people won't challenge you unless you are making ridiculous claims.

To find articles for your use, look at www.articlesbase.com, www.articlecircle.com, www.findarticles.com, and a host of others. One my favorites is www.ezinearticles.com.

If you have recently joined a company with a great reputation, use their credibility as a spring board for your own. Instead of talking about yourself, brag about the company. "I'm a million dollar producer" then becomes, "My company closed $145 Million in the first quarter. Wouldn't you like to do business with that kind of success?"

Being a published writer is one of the best ways to gain credibility. I have scores of published articles on various subjects even though I didn't consider myself a "writer" for a long period of time.

I once wrote a real estate column in my local business paper. I didn't get any pay, but I did get my picture and contact information in the hands of thousands of people. The fact that I was a "columnist" gave me more credibility.

Fox News', Bret Hume observed, "In the end, you make your reputation and you have your success based upon credibility and being able to provide people who are really hungry for information they want."

Learn to write. It's not that difficult. You can even hire people to write for you or, record a class you teach and have it transcribed and edited.

Submit your articles on line and you are an expert. Just be sure to provide good, solid content. Don't hold back. Content is king.

Now, go make it a great credibility kind of day.

36

Simplicity – A Great Way to Live

Possessing an entrepreneurial spirit, I sometimes find myself knee deep in busy business clutter. That's the stuff that goes on around me that doesn't result in better relationships, more business productivity, a more solid spiritual undergirding, or having my body in better physical shape.

I think it's interesting that many times we confuse "busy" with "growing." We think that if we stay busy, our relationships will blossom, our business will flourish, we will evolve into spiritual giants, and a six pack will develop where flab now overshadows our waistline.

It comes as a big surprise for some to learn that busy doesn't mean better. Activity doesn't necessarily mean positive, forward action. In many cases, "busy" simply means distractions and interruptions from more important things.

Over the years I've learned that we can get so busy doing good things that we don't have any time left over the BEST things.

Feeling the exhilaration of success is not really complicated. In fact, it really boils down to a few simple rules. So, here's my Seven Simple Rules for Success.

1. Keep things simple. Sometimes we fail to move forward because we have elaborate plans that are difficult or impossible to work through. In your business, make sure your systems are practical and easy to follow. If your plan is too complicated, you'll nurture frustration and quit before you reach your goal.

2. Prioritize - Step 1. As stated earlier, just because there are good things to do, doesn't mean they are the best things for you to do. The secret in living a quality life is found in the choices you make. Make a list of things that are important to you. Then, have a goal of cultivating those important things.

3. Prioritize Step - 2. Work off a daily check list and you will be amazed at how much you can get done. Number one on my daily list is the thing I really don't want to do that day. I do it first so I can check it off my list (if I don't, I tend to dread it all day). Then, I work down my list until I'm done.

4. If you're in business, spend at least one uninterrupted hour of prospecting each day. Prospecting is the one daily activity that will usually guarantee success; without it, you will fail – no question. Do not take calls, book appointments, go to Starbucks, chat at the office cooler, or wrestle with paperwork. No other activity is more important to your overall business success.

5. Plan and adapt. A plan is simply a rough road map that defines where you want to be within a specific time frame. Break down your goal into daily activity, and

then focus on that. As circumstances change, make corrections and adjustments, but keep moving forward.

6. Limit your focus. You cannot be all things to all people. As a result, you need to define a specific niche market in which to focus and be an expert. I work my niche market and refer out (for a fee to others in my profession) those who fail to fit in my niche. In my 30 plus years in business I've learned that I make more money and I have more free time when I work this way. I also reduce the risk of a lawsuit, too, because I'm not working outside my area of expertise.

7. Limit your number of clients. Let's face it, as lovable as you are, there are some people with whom you cannot work. I try to eliminate the prospective clients very quickly. When I talk with a prospective client, it's really <u>my interview</u> to determine if I think we are good fit. If I feel we are wrong for each other, I refer them (again, for a fee) to someone in my profession I believe would benefit the prospective client. It's better to make a little money later in a referral fee than to spend my money, time and emotional output on a project I deem income challenged.

Henry David Thoreau said, "Simplicity, simplicity, simplicity! I say, let your affairs be as two or three, and not a hundred or a thousand, instead of a million count half a dozen, and keep your accounts on your thumb-nail."

Now, keep your life simple and make it a great day.

Life is full of beauty. Notice it.

Notice the bumble bee, the small child,

and the smiling faces. Smell the rain,

and feel the wind.

Live your life to the fullest potential,

and fight for your dreams.
Ashley Smith

37

Storms of Doubt

I've talked to many people who are experiencing very rough financial storms. In many cases, events out of their control have resulted in the evaporation of life savings, home foreclosures and shrinking income (if any income at all).

Where once there was a feeling of security and confidence there is now insecurity and feelings of helplessness as the storm of doubt has filled the psyche and hearts of once secure people.

In light of the financial challenges of 2010, I offer positive input in hope that your "reality" can be improved upon. Since you are reading this I assume you want to believe in the future - and I want to help you believe.

The principles presented here are focused on financial issues but they also apply to doubt wherever it may appear in your life. So, let's start here:

Doubt is, among other things, a feeling of uncertainty or being unconvinced about the future. This subjective feeling we get is sometimes worthy of our attention.

You have already read about my fall from a roof. If you recall, there was a short in the electrical wiring and I spent a long period recovering serious contusions and broken vertebra. Here's what I didn't tell you: It took me several months to have enough courage to turn on a light switch (and even longer to pull the trigger on a skill saw). Doubt in the safety of electrical equipment caused me to drown in fear. Once I gained the confidence to turn on a light switch (without another excursion to a hospital emergency room), I could move forward as the fear eventually faded way.

The cure for doubt is to simply take action. John Kanary, an expert at increasing effectiveness and unlocking potential correctly observed: "If doubt is challenging you and you do not act, doubts will grow. Challenge the doubts with action and you will grow. Doubt and action are incompatible."

I have also shared with you how that in my early 20s I started a direct sales company, selling a high priced safety item for home use. I had a terrible speech impediment at the time and I was consumed with doubt which resulted in fear about knocking on a new door or making a telephone call. Once I simply jumped in and did the activity that was needed for success, I discovered my doubt and fear were not valid "feelings." And the power in this example lies in the fact that if you take action and move forward, you will discover the same thing.

Below you will find what I believe is the secret in the finding peace in your storm of doubt and the confidence to move forward. I also believe when you follow these steps you will discover a power which flows from within when you take action.

This is how you find power in the storm of your skepticism:

1. Based upon your belief system, honestly face your doubt by asking if it's rational and/or valid. If your doubt contradicts your belief system, recognize that fact and take action by moving forward.

2. Focus on good things. As a friend of mine is fond of saying, you can only think about one thing at a time. Choose the good and noble things. Recall a time when someone did something nice for you and remember how that made you feel. Think about your past successes. What did you do right? Why were you a success?

3. Appreciate that you were not specifically chosen for experiencing a financial disaster. Sometimes life simply throws things our way so that we can be better prepared for better times ahead. There have always been corrections in market conditions and there will be more in the future.

4. Stop feeling sorry for yourself. As long as you are thinking about how tough times are for you, you will not move forward. Get beyond that point by giving some thought on how you might be able to help someone else.

5. Make a plan and take action. You cannot change the past but you can mold tomorrow. Set some good short term, midterm, and long term goals. Then, break down those goals into daily activity. As you go about your day, focus on taking action on the daily activity.

6. Plan to give! That's right! I know things are not so pleasant right now, so think about giving. You have to

mentally and spiritually move off center stage and put something or someone else there.

7. When you experience doubt, don't let guilt take over. Doubt is okay if we learn to use it to construct a solid framework around our lives. Choose to build a fortress by challenging your doubt with action.

Now, find power in your storm of doubt and move forward. This is YOUR day. Make it a great one.

38

A Lesson from Chicken Little

Do you remember the children's fairy tale about Chicken Little? The tale begins:

> "Once upon a time there was a tiny, tiny chicken named Chicken Little. One day Chicken Little was scratching in the garden when something fell on her head.
>
> "Oh," cried Chicken Little, "the sky is falling. I must go tell the king."'

In fact, the sky wasn't falling at all but she immediately drew the worst possible conclusion. Have you ever done something similar? Like Chicken Little, all of us have had something happen and assumed the worst.

From personal experience, I know how easy it is to fall into that trap. Unfortunately, thinking the worst and negative thinking are deadly traps. Consider another familiar folk tale featuring Brer Rabbit.

If you recall, the result of his uncontrolled negative emotion and thought was that he became trapped in a mess of his own making – stuck to Tar Baby – unable to avoid being physically controlled by his nemesis, Brer Fox. That's what negative thinking does. It puts the power in someone else's hands and renders us helpless.

To break free from our evolving Tar Baby (negative thoughts, negative self talk, negative relationships, negative life, etc.), we are compelled to look past the negative. Surely, we are supposed to learn lessons from past failures and hurts, but then we must choose to move forward and focus on the positive possibilities if we are to succeed.

The fundamental difference between those who are successful (however you define it) and those who are not, is, to a large degree, the way we think about and view events. While the negative thinker more often sees peril, the positive one more often sees opportunity. When you choose the latter, you are able to transform your frustration, fear and anxiety - and all the energy that goes into those – into a determination that will take you to the next level.

Chicken Little felt something, or thought she did. Was it the sky falling? No! But she wasted a lot of time and energy on that emotional notion. I think she missed a wonderful opportunity and failed to appreciate a blessing. Unfortunately, we will never know what that was because of her focused fear.

Brer Rabbit's uncontrolled emotional outbursts at perceived insults and/or perceived lack of respect due him brought him face to face with his own demise – lunch for a hungry wolf. Brer Rabbit could have easily avoided the danger if he had accurately assessed the situation.

What benefits are you missing because of the way you think? It matters little that you have fears and failures. We all do. What matters is the way you look at them, assess them, and react. Reacting positively and with expectation is the single most important ingredient in the formula for your success.

My suggestion is to learn the much needed lessons life tosses your way, work on eliminating negative emotion, and live a positive, energy filled life. I often write about the following principles but they're worth repeating. Here are six principles that will help you accomplish the goal of a positive, energy filled life:

1. Mentally manage your responses. Recognize that most things are out of your control. Change those things you can, and for those things you cannot change, redirect your negative thoughts so that they will not control you.

2. Recognize that fear is a normal part of humanness. Face your fears head on, as difficult as it may be, and move forward. Once you are past them, you will be exhilarated.

3. When you "feel" slighted or disrespected, understand that the vast majority of the time you are not the focus. To be honest, people give you very little thought and their inappropriate and thoughtless action and words say more about them than it does you.

4. Avoid using negative and harsh words. Anyone can spout off and use words and actions that demonstrate bad choices. You can show your sense of accomplishment when you rise above the fray and avoid verbal mud wrestling. Think good, positive things. It's your choice.

5.   Avoid negative thinkers and selectively build a positive support team or master mind group. A positive group of like minded people is a tremendous asset.

6.   Look for opportunity. If, as the saying goes, you are handed a lemon, find a way to sell lemonade. It's up to you to decide if the situation leaves you with a sour taste or you enjoy sweat taste success.

Am I always successful with the above? Frankly, no! Sometimes I struggle when things get really personal and I fall far short of my goal. I also find that in the struggle I may use words and actions that I would rather not use. When that happens, I have the unpleasant task of trying to make amends. Sometimes I can and sometimes I can't. When I can't, I have to accept personal responsibility and live with my bad choice.

But I want you to know that I have come a long, long way since I was young and eager to correct the injustices and hurtful things I perceived as personal attacks.

I want you to join me in embracing the principles above by embracing effective, unstoppable determination as we press forward. Let's discover positive possibilities on our way to true freedom and success.

Now go make it a "possibility" day.

39

Money is Just an Idea

I read a book that caught my attention several years ago. At the time, it was relatively new in the market place and the first of several books in a series. The little known author was Robert Kiyosaki and the book was "Rich Dad, Poor Dad."

Kiyoisaki is now world famous - the "Rich Dad" series have sold multiple millions of copies and is a worldwide brand. Although there is nothing new about the principles shared in this worthwhile read, I did learn some things that made a difference for me.

One quote I picked up and use from "Rich Dad, Poor Dad" is: "Money is just an idea." I like that quote and it is something I believe!

Recently a friend challenged my thinking when I used it: "That may be the dumbest thing you have ever said. 'Money is just an idea' is simply baloney," he barked. "There is no way having an idea will pay the rent or put gas in the car."

Can money and wealth be just one idea away? Yes, it can and I will share with you how you can find that to be true.

First, however, I want you to understand what it ***does not*** mean: You will not find $100,000 in cash on your nightstand when you wake up one morning with a great idea or two.

The points that follow are the foundational principles you need if you truly want your ideas to turn green (the color of money). After a solid foundation is constructed, you can build on it by gaining specific information, building a solid business model, developing marketing know-how, dotting your "I's" and crossing your "T's" - all of which are subjects for other written pieces.

Here are the foundational principles for today:

1. **Good personal relationships** - I've never seen anyone bring up the subject of good relationships in this context. But good personal relationships with your spouse or close friends are needed.

   We are beings that need others. Without this ingredient you will always be looking for something more because you instinctually know something is missing. Besides, people in your sphere of relationships may help fund and/or market your idea.

2. **Good social skills** - We do not succeed in a vacuum. Social skills will help you make contacts that can help transform your idea into a reality.

   "Networking" is a trendy word now, but it's also a needed ability. The good news is, networking can be learned. There are books available on the subject that can help you become more of a social networking person. Pick up two or three and get some good ideas on how to build social contacts and turn those social contacts into assets. Then, put into action what you learn.

Here's why: One theory suggests that you are only six people removed from someone who has what you need. Do you need money, information, ideas, support, or any other thing? Good social networking skills will open doors that will provide answers you require.

3. **Spiritual Balance** - This area of our lives is often overlooked or avoided in much of the information written on the subject of success.

Here's rock-solid truth: When we are out of balance spiritually, we start believing that we are the center of the universe and everything revolves around us. That kind of thinking leads to an empty, shallow existence. Or, we start believing we are unworthy of anything thing good. The latter results in lack of effort and a lack of motivation to move forward.

We are spiritual beings and benefit from time scheduled for spiritual "exercise" - just like we do from physical exercise. How will you build "spiritual biceps," and develop a more balanced life, without focused effort for spiritual equilibrium? You may contact me if you want to learn more about this.

4. **Financial basics** - Turning your ideas into money will take some basic understanding of accounting and how money works. When I started my first brick and mortar business at the age of 20, I didn't know if I had $5 or $500.

My advice to anyone wanting financial success is to take a local community college course (or self directed study) on basic accounting principles. There are also accounting software packages available that will assist you keeping good books, too.

Money is just an idea away. But, you have to get in gear and go to work by defining in writing what you want to accomplish. Then, describe what you think you have to do to get there. After that, break down your goals into daily activity and **_DO_** the activity each day.

Kiyosaki also wrote: "The size of your success is measured by the strength of your desire; the size of your dream; and how you handle disappointment along the way."

As you move forward, you will need to make adjustments as new problems and disappointments pop up (and they surely will). Ultimately, if you work smart, you can realize your dreams by turning your ideas into money.

Now go make your dreams come true.

40

Consider the Flea

When you rolled out of bed this morning I'm sure you asked: How high can a flee jump? No? Me either. But, I found myself face-to-face with the answer to this fascinating question. Being somewhat creative, I wondered how I could use this useful and valuable information. So I did a little research.

Insecta Inspecta World states: ". . . The flea when jumping accelerates 50 times faster than a space shuttle. Although fleas cannot fly, they can jump over seven inches high and thirteen inches long, that is about one hundred and fifty times its own length. Without its outer shell it would get smashed by the velocity of the jump, and especially on its landing...."

Amazing as it sounds, when fleas are put into a container (as in a small jar or drinking glass), the little rascals will literally jump out. If you place a sheet of paper over the top of the container, the fleas will jump up and hit the sheet of paper then fall back to the bottom.

Here's what's really interesting: After several failed attempts to jump out of the container, the fleas are "mentally reconditioned" and will only leap as high the sheet of paper – **even after the paper has been removed**. Their previous reality has been replaced with a new one that limits their performance.

That's a worthy lesson for us to mull over. I believe many of us, based on personal experiences, are held in place (in our business endeavors, spiritual growth, personal development, personal relationships, etc.) by our own self imposed limits.

In some behavior, we are like fleas. For example, we were jumping high, but we got hit hard by the economy (out of our control) and experienced difficult times. Understand that there is no physical barrier. But lots of folk carry on as though there is a ceiling that prevents them from breaking out and experiencing any kind of new reality.

Like the flea, some high level performers learned that jumping high meant getting the snot kicked out of them, so they made mental adjustments to lessen the pain. The heartbreaking side effect of that choice is that they have also limited the hope for future high level performance.

The current (2010) economic climate…, well…, sucks. Most of the people I know have lost huge sums of money and equity. I know I have lost millions. A lot of people I know have filed for bankruptcy protection. I even know people who have committed suicide over (I presume) the loss of money, credibility, a spouse and family.

My heart truly goes out to those who feel despair. I'm empathetic - I truly feel their pain. But now, faced with the economic challenges before them, many of my friends and acquaintances have limited their options by constructing the mental barriers I previously referred to.

They are like the fleas that will not jump out of the uncovered container. The result is, not knowing what else to do, they ask fellow fleas, "How do we break free? How can we move forward? How do we get out of this mess? How can we succeed?"

Here's a valuable principal founded on truth:

If you want to go to escape your current limitations and feel the exhilaration found in the next level (in whatever discipline or interest you choose), don't ask your fellow fleas what to do. If they held the answers for breaking free from the limits they now embrace, they wouldn't be in your position. In a worst case scenario, they will keep you from moving toward success by unconsciously doing their best to hold you where they are. Remember - misery loves company.

If you truly want to disentangle yourself from the tentacles of a limited belief system, and if you want to experience freedom from your self imposed limits, seek out those whom are not limited by your mental obstacles. Find someone, a mentor, who is where you want to be. That person can help you much more than fellow fleas sharing the same limited mindset.

Word of Caution: Thinking outside the box, and acting outside the box, may cost you some friends. Most of your fellow fleas will want you to stay within the boundaries of their comfort zone. They will say, in a variety of ways, words that project the idea: "You can't do that!"

When you are free of those self imposed boundaries, your "friends" may well reject you because you will not share the same mental altitude anymore. But that's okay. Move forward.

Here's what I suggest:

1. Clearly define where you want to be.

2. Answer This: Who can help you get there?" and "What am I willing to give in return?

3. Set some target dates for successes.

4. Define how you will get there.

5. Work your plan and make adjustments as needed.

6. Associates with those not limited with your mindset.

7. Take one other flea with you on your journey.

It's now up to you. What will you do? Whatever your choice, you have chosen a path. Robert Frost concludes his famous "The Road Not Taken" by writing:

> "I shall be telling this with a sigh
> "Somewhere ages and ages hence:
> "Two roads diverged in a wood, and I --
> "I took the one less travelled by,
> "and that has made all the difference."

I challenge to you is to take the "road less traveled" and shred the paper barrier.

Make it a superior day.

Here's The Rest

There you have it! I hope you have enjoyed and benefited from our time together.

As a way of saying, "Thank You" for taking this journey with me, I offer you a free newsletter that can help keep you on track. Send me an email at SignMeUp@DonLoyd.com (type "Sign Me Up" in the subject line) and I will include you in my mailing list.

My newsletter is a source of encouragement, inspiration and motivation. You will also be able to keep track of my speaking engagements.

If you would like to book me for a speaking event (I have spoken publicly to large and small audiences more than 2,000 times – not too bad for a guy who could barely talk!), you may contact me at DonaldLoyd@Gmail.com. I have a compelling story and a few open dates.

Do me a favor.

If you were blessed, helped or encouraged by this work, please send me an email and tell me how you benefited, how your life has changed, how you were inspired, or whatever message you would like to send. I may use your comments online. Email me at DonaldLoyd@Gmail.com.

Now, what are you waiting for? Make it an awe-inspiring life.

CPSIA information can be obtained
at www.ICGtesting.com
Printed in the USA
BVHW03s1953090518
515756BV00030B/498/P